So, You Wanna

Be A

Writer?

Published by
Beyond Words Publishing, Inc.
20827 NW Cornell Road, Suite 500
Hillsboro, Oregon 97124
503-531-8700
www.beyondword.com

The information contained in this book is intended to be educational and not for diagnosis, prescription, or treatment of mental and/or physical health disorders, whatsoever. This information should not replace competent medical and/or psychological care. The authors and publisher are in no way liable for any use or misuse of the information.

ISBN: 1-58270-043-5

Editors: Michelle Roehm McCann and Emily Strelow
Interior Art: Laura Eldridge and Corey Mistretta
Design: Andrea Boven / Boven Design Studio, Inc.
Proofreader: Susan Beal
Printed in the United States of America
Distributed to the book trade by Publishers Group West

"About Wishing" Copyright © 2001 by Matthew Stepanek
"Angel-Wings" Copyright © 2001 by Matthew Stepanek

Library of Congress Cataloging-in-Publication Data

Hambleton, Vicki.
  So, you wanna be a writer? : how to write, get published, and maybe even make it big! / written by Vicki Hambleton and Cathleen Greenwood.
        p. cm. — (So, you wanna be …)
        ISBN 1-58270-043-5 (pbk.)
    1. Authorship—Juvenile literature. 2. Authorship—marketing—Juvenile literature. [1. Authorship—Vocational guidance. 2. Vocational guidance.] I. Greenwood, Cathleen. II. Title. III. Series.

PN159 .H28 2001
808'.02—dc21   2001018423

The corporate mission of Beyond Words Publishing, Inc: *Inspire to Integrity*

So, You Wanna Be A Writer?

BY VICKI HAMBLETON & CATHLEEN GREENWOOD
featuring 10 Real Kid Authors!

BEYOND
WORDS
Publishing
I N C

contents

CHAPTER 1

What's It Like to Be a Writer?

You pull into the parking lot of your favorite bookstore, knowing that this time it's not going to be just to meet your buddies for a frappucino. Someone else is expecting you—YOUR FANS! You keep your sunglasses on as you walk in the front door, head down, but the manager recognizes you anyway. You are whisked away to the Green Room, offered the brand of bottled water your characters are famous for drinking, and escorted to "The Book Signing Table." It's covered with a red velvet cloth, piled high with copies of YOUR book, and there are scores of fans jostling for position behind the velvet ropes to make sure they get their books signed by the author—YOU!

Cameras flash, your smile dazzles, you whip out your favorite pen, and start signing as fast as you can, murmuring words of gratitude in response to the exclamations of love and adulation from each reader.

Is this what it's like to be a writer? You bet! Okay, maybe it's not *always* like this—but it does happen. And, believe it or not, it can happen to you, especially if you start thinking of yourself as a writer now, and doing the things real writers do. This book will help you—we promise.

Keep that thrilling, ultimate scenario in mind, but let's get a bit more realistic for a few minutes. Look over the list below and circle what you really think it's like to be a writer:

1. lonely
2. cool
3. strange
4. incredibly exciting
5. hard work
6. not like real work at all
7. boring
8. a life of riches
9. a life of poverty
10. people love you
11. people think you're a geek
12. fun
13. frustrating
14. fantastic
15. scary
16. hilarious
17. eeeyew!

- If you circled just **even numbers** (2,4,6,8, etc…), we love you! You have a positive attitude about writing. And you're right… being a writer CAN BE all of those things! (Although, to be honest, not *all* the time.)
- If you circled just **odd numbers** (1,3,5,7, etc …), you're right too. Being a writer can be tough, but it's NEVER as bad as that whole list. At least, not if you read this book first!
- If you circled **all** the items on the list, you are right on target—being a writer is often like *all* of these things, at one point or another.

How One Author Got His Start

We asked **Michael Crichton** to tell us about how he got started as a writer. Believe it or not, the creator of *Jurassic Park* and the TV show *ER* first got published when he was a kid.

When did you know you wanted to be a writer?

My father was a journalist, so I grew up seeing him type to earn a living. His example made writing seem like a normal thing to do. I was attracted to writing from an early age, and did a lot of it. I wrote for my high school and town newspaper, and for the college newspaper. Later on, in medical school, I started writing novels to pay my way through school.

I was fourteen years old when I published my first piece. On a family vacation I visited Sunset Crater Volcano National Monument in Arizona, and I thought it was pretty interesting, and that more people should know about it. My parents said that the Sunday *New York Times* travel section published articles by readers, and suggested I write an article for the paper. So I sent in an essay—and they published it. I was very excited.

What advice would you give a young writer?

I always tell writers to write. If you think you're interested in writing, just start writing. Write extra compositions for school assignments. Write for the school paper, the yearbook, or the town newspaper. Write articles. Write poetry. Write plays. Write anything you have a mind to, but write a lot.

This will help you learn how to do it—I believe writers are invariably self-taught. But equally important, you'll also find out if you really like writing as much as you think you do. Although writing can be very satisfying, it's a hard job, and a peculiar one. You've got to be self-disciplined, and you've got to tolerate being alone a lot. It's a great life, but it's not for everyone.

If you like to write, you are one of the luckiest people in the world. Writers shape thoughts into words and those words can inspire, motivate, teach, and entertain those who read them. Have you ever read something that made you cry? *Black Beauty, Walk Two Moons* or *Charlotte's Web*? Or maybe a story in a magazine about a terrible famine? How about something that made you angry? Scared? Happy? How about a book that you just couldn't put down and had to finish under the covers long after midnight…perhaps a Harry Potter tale?

All of these stories started with writers. There are as many different kinds of writers as there are stories to tell. Writers don't just write books, either. When you watch ESPN to catch the sports scores, the reporters on those shows read scripts written by writers. Or when you watch your favorite sitcom…a writer did that as well. There are novelists, poets, playwrights, screenwriters, reporters, medical writers, and technical writers, just to name a few. And the good news is that you can make a living as a writer. Your writing can take you all over the world if you choose, or you can create books in the comfort of your own home—even in your PJs, if you want!

If you like to write, you can use your talent to try lots of different things. All it takes is a desire to write and pen and paper…or a laptop. Throughout the book, you'll hear from lots of different kinds of writers, including kids just like you, about what they do, how they got there, and why they love writing.

WHAT'S NEXT FOR YOU?

What do the following writers have in common with Michael Crichton?

Sylvia Plath

James Joyce

Edgar Allen Poe

Langston Hughes
F. Scott Fitzgerald
Louisa May Alcott
Ernest Hemingway
Walt Whitman
Stephen King
Cameron Crowe
S.E. Hinton

If you guessed that they all published their writing while they were teenagers, you're right! They didn't wait until they were adults to go for their dreams and become writers, and you don't need to either. Add *your* name to this list! There are so many kinds of writing to try, and so many ways to get published as a kid, why wait?

Inspired? Read on and find out how you can get started right now!

Amelia Atwater-Rhodes, age 16

What's it like to be a popular teen author? We asked Amelia Atwater-Rhodes, author of *In the Forests of the Night* and *Demon in My View* to find out. At only thirteen, she wrote her first novel, *In the Forests of the Night,* but never dreamed it would be published. On her fourteenth birthday, she found out that her first novel was accepted for publication. What a birthday present! Here's what she has to say about writing:

Where do you get your inspiration? Everywhere. Things friends will say, things I see, characters that intrigue me.

How do you come up with your ideas? I start with a minor character, then expand on that character. In the first book I ever wrote, I just threw together everyone I knew, scanty plot line, flat characters. I just wrote to pass the time. That book will never *ever* be published (she says, laughing). Eventually, I wanted to know more about the characters I'd created. The first things I wrote weren't very good, but they did get me started writing, which was important.

Have you had anything else published before your first novel? *In the Forests of the Night* was the first thing I had published. My sister's English teacher, Tom Hart, happened to be a literary agent as well. A friend bragged about me to him and he asked to see my books. He submitted my manuscript to a few houses, and Doubleday took it.

How has your writing evolved? Every book I write, I get more into it. History is one of my passions right now. Sometimes I'll take inspiration from characters in Ancient Egypt, Rome, or Mesoamerica. My first characters were flat, but now they're more complex. Some of my characters now I feel I know really well. I know them like best friends, sometimes better.

How did it feel the first time you were published? It came as a shock. The first time I saw my book in print I could barely believe it. I had to tell myself this is real, I'm not dreaming.

What does your writing space look like? I mostly write on the computer in my room (which is, of course, trashed). I can write anywhere as long as it's quiet. I also do writing and character sketches in notebooks.

How do you make time for your writing? Writing is one of those things that you will make time for if you want to do it. When I have something to write, I'll need to write it, whether it's staying up till 3 a.m. or jotting it down in the middle of Physics. If you love writing, you will make time for it.

Do you think reading helps writing? Definitely. I can't understand when people say they like to write, but not read. When you read, you get used to visualizing things in print. I'm not a big television/movie fan, so I always have spent a lot of time reading. You learn to see things in words. You figure out how to express yourself in words. It becomes like another sense. Reading teaches you the mechanics and logistics, like vocab and structure, that are important to writing. You learn the basics, then get the ideas for your writing. It's like people who listen to music a lot, they'll eventually want to sing.

What's your advice for aspiring kid writers? Go out and do it. Find other people who write. When I found other people who wrote, I felt more comfortable about myself. Keep at it! You can always edit. Every author is his or her own worst critic. If you love to write, just do it.

CHAPTER 2

Getting Started with the "Write" Stuff: Time, Tools, and Turf

*S*occer practice, e-mails from friends, feeding the dog, cleaning your room, ...not to mention the dreaded H-word: HOMEWORK! You are already sooooo busy—how could you ever squeeze in time for writing?

Not to mention, your computer is a piece of junk and you share a room with your sister/brother/pet cobra lunching on live mice. How are you supposed to create a brilliant piece of writing when you can't even hear yourself think half the time?

Does this sound familiar? Lots of writers know they want to write, but mysteriously find themselves sidetracked. To get started, there are a few things you will want to set up to help you avoid getting sidetracked when you should be writing, also known as the "Three Ts": Time, Tools, and Turf. The fact is, the hardest part of writing can be those first steps: making the time to do it, getting the writing materials you need ready to go, and finding a good place to write. Once you get over these first hurdles and actually start scribbling or typing real words, you *are* a writer.

Famous writers often have famous habits that help them write. Victor Hugo made his servant lock him in a room until he finished some writing. Ernest Hemingway marched upstairs every morning to his writing room, unlocking the door only to let in one of his six-toed cats!

Hopefully you won't have to lock yourself alone in a room to be a writer, but there are some things you can do that will make getting started easier for you. Try using earplugs to block out the noise of your house. Or, have an honest chat with your family about needing some space and time. It might help to tell them that you plan to work for a specific amount of time—say, one hour—instead of just a general "can you be quiet forever" kind of request. You may be pleasantly surprised at how willing your family is to support you in doing something as important as writing…if you just ask.

Once you have decided to start writing, tell yourself that no one needs to read what you write—the important thing is to get words on paper (or computer). It doesn't really matter what comes out—real writers admit that they write tons of junk, but that's where they find the good stuff that turns into their best writing later. Here are some suggestions to help you get started. (Hint: Turn off the TV first!)

FINDING THE "WRITE" TIME

Some writers like to set aside large chunks of time every day for their writing. Stephen King, for example, writes eight hours a day, every day of the year. The only days he takes off are his birthday, Christmas, and the Fourth of July!

But, you don't *have* to give up your entire social life to be a writer. In fact, writing doesn't even have to take up large blocks of time, like school writing assignments. When you get hungry for some food, you eat, right? And sometimes a little snack is the perfect thing. Well, when you get hungry to write, you should write!

And, it can be "snack" writing—a little bit here, a little bit there. Try scheduling a short "before breakfast" writing snack, limiting yourself to ten or twenty minutes. You could use a book of poetry (Robert Frost or Emily Dickinson work well), and respond to one line a day.

As you go through your day, when you see something or get an idea for writing, take a writing "snack" and jot yourself a quick note. Sometimes these are seeds that you can expand on later. Promise yourself to write something every day, or every other day, or even just once a week—even if it's only a few lines. Pretty soon, your writing practices will get you in better shape as a writer, and your appetite for writing will grow. A little "snack" won't be enough any more, and you'll find yourself stretching out your morning sessions or scheduling longer sessions just before bed or after basketball practice. Before you know it, you'll actually start looking forward to your writing sessions!

COLLECTING THE "WRITE" TOOLS

One of the best things about writing is that you don't need a bunch of expensive gear to do it. Whether you're listing ideas in a journal or typing up that last chapter of your brilliant novel, you deserve to use tools that work for you. But, that doesn't mean you have to have a whole new room or a bunch of expensive supplies either. Your writing tool box just needs to include things that help your writing.

Choosing something to write *in* is a good place to start. You might like a hardcover marble composition book because you can use it without a desk. Or, you might prefer a spiral-bound notebook, with or without lines. Think about size—does it need to be light so you can carry it in your backpack, small to fit in your pocket, or will it stay at home on your desk? Do you like big fat pages where your

10

thoughts can wander, or small pages that are easy to fill? Do you like writing in pencil or ink? Think about what makes you comfortable while writing, and choose your journal and paper and writing instruments with those preferences in mind.

CREATING THE "WRITE" TURF

Next, think about *where* you like to write. At a desk? Lying on the floor? In your favorite chair? On the computer? No matter where, you should find a spot that's open and inviting for you, and where all of your writing tools are easily available. Keep your writing "turf" clear and clean, so picking up junk won't sidetrack you when you are ready to write. You deserve a space of your own for writing that is so encouraging that you smile when you see it and *want* to get started.

To make the space your own, be creative. Why not decorate? Plenty of writers put up inspiring quotes, pictures, posters, etc. in their writing spaces to help keep their creativity going. Decorating is a way to mark your writing "turf" clearly for all to see. When you are sitting there, you'll be sending the signal "Writer at Work!"—to yourself and to your family. It's not hard to make your writing space happen; just make sure that all of the following items are there waiting for you in your special place:

Writing Stuff Checklist:
- ✓ favorite pens/pencils
- ✓ favorite paper/journal/notebook/typewriter/computer
- ____ gluestick (not necessary, but great for pasting important tidbits into your journal)
- ✓ file folders (not necessary, but handy for keeping your different writing projects organized)
- ____ headphones/earmuffs/earplugs (not necessary, but nice for

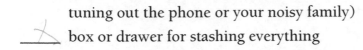
tuning out the phone or your noisy family)

box or drawer for stashing everything

TIPS FOR COLLECTING THE "WRITE" IDEAS

√ *Journaling*

Who needs a journal? You do! If you plan to write and sound real (or even *unreal*), there is no greater source for ideas and words than real life. It's important to keep a journal and to write in it every day. What you write does not have to make sense or be perfect—just try to record what you notice. Each time you look through your journal, you won't believe how many ideas and words and phrases you can use from it.

Some writers use journals as diaries, and record their daily activities and thoughts in them. This can be a great way for you to start thinking about your world and making sense of it. A diary/journal can be a great best friend, always ready to listen, always forgiving, never judgmental. If you like this idea, you might want to give your journal a name, like Anne Frank did. At first, Anne just listed the day's activities in her new diary, but after she named the diary "Kitty," she began writing in it as if she were writing to a person. The diary became a true friend Anne could share her hopes, fears and dreams with. And as you probably know already, that diary also became one of the most powerful books ever written.

You don't always have to *write* in a journal—you can sketch and draw, or even use scrapbook techniques. Writers use journals as memory-joggers, so keep a gluestick handy and paste in movie stubs, photos from magazines, great newspaper headlines … anything that strikes you. If you contribute to it every day, pretty soon you'll find yourself looking back over your entries and discovering a goldmine of ideas and language to use in your writing.

Observing

Writers have lots of different ways they keep journals. Some write long, rambling paragraphs, some list short thoughts, some copy down words or phrases they overhear. Good writers make readers feel as if they are on the scene, observing and becoming part of the story. Good writers must learn to observe and write about what they see, hear, and feel. Hang around, listen, pay attention— and be sure to write it all down. You *think* you'll remember the comment that jerk made in the cafeteria, but you won't when you need it for a villain's remark in your next story!

You can actually go on little "spy trips" with your journal, observing your world and writing down what you see. Look at what's in front of you as if it were a scene in a movie; keep an eye peeled for interesting characters, and write how they act and move, as well as what they say. Write down how the sky looks or how the air smells in that particular setting. Jot down scraps of conversation—nothing is more real than reality. Only you can know the best spots for "spy trips" in your area, but here are some good general places for observing human behavior: a crowded park, the school cafeteria, a city bus or subway, the local mall…hey, your very own kitchen at dinnertime is the perfect place to watch a "normal" family in action!

Reading!

Now here's a big secret for you: almost all great writers *love* to read! That's often how they got interested in writing in the first place. And it's not unusual for a writer of one kind of book (say, sci-fi) to prefer reading completely different kinds of books (say, poetry).The point is that reading is a huge *resource* for you as a writer. Reading will help you find words, phrases, topics, characters, style, and phrasing for your own writing.

ARCHETYPES—
HAVEN'T I HEARD THAT STORY SOMEWHERE BEFORE...

Since the dawn of time when humans first began telling stories in caves, the same types of plots and characters have appeared over and over again. The more you read, the more you'll notice how authors reuse these same models or "archetypes."

There is the archetype "hero," (Bilbo Baggins, Luke Skywalker, Alice in Wonderland, Meg from *A Wrinkle in Time*, Harry Potter) a lonely character who doesn't think he/she is good enough to be a hero. In the archetype "hero story," the heroes leave on a perilous journey, meet some buddies to help them in their adventures, and finally triumph in the end using their courage and cleverness.

Fairy tales are full of archetype characters: the "innocent victim" (Snow White, Cinderella, Little Red Riding Hood) who is preyed on by a "villain" (wicked stepmothers, evil sorcerers, hungry old ladies living in candy houses) and rescued in the end by the "good guy/gal" (handsome prince, fairy godmother, brave woodsman).

There are lots of interesting character archetypes and story archetypes repeated in great literature. Watch out for them in your reading, and then you can decide which pieces of these tried-and-true models you might want to use in *your* writing.

Reading is also a great way to "check out the competition." In most jobs, people have to "research" what others in their field are doing. No problem for writers—all you have to do is read to find out what other writers are up to. Once you start writing in your journal and taking yourself seriously as a writer, you will find yourself reading with new eyes. You'll start to notice how other writers deal with things you're wondering about, such as character development, setting description or use of metaphor.

If you know what type of writing you want to do (poetry, horror, etc.), reading that kind of book will really help you get started. No one is expected to learn a craft without first seeing samples of the finished product. How could a boat builder construct a sailboat if she had never even seen one before? So, consider reading part of a writer's job—part of *your* job—and one of the best parts!

Reading is especially good to do when you're stuck in your writing. A really good book will take you on a little vacation to other worlds that renew your creativity and excitement about writing. Giving your brain a vacation by reading is often just what you need to get started writing again.

Book Clubs

Believe it or not, there are lots of other kids out there who love to read…and they are a fantastic resource for you as a writer. Joining a book club will introduce you to new books, friends who share your passion, and tons of great writing ideas—not just from the books, but from the club members as well. Ask a librarian at school or at your local library for clubs in your area. When you find one, check out the list of books they've read in the past few meetings to see if they interest you. This is a good way to see if that club's reading choices will fit with yours.

Book clubs not only open you up to new kinds of writing and authors, but they are also your golden opportunity to see how readers react to different kinds of writing and to find out what they like and don't like about various stories, styles and techniques. Some day people will be reading *your* writing and your book club experiences will remind you to keep your future audience in mind when you write.

If you can't find a book club, just start your own—all it takes is one other person! Here's how they work:

1. Agree on a regular meeting place, day, and time (like the first Wednesday of the month at 4:30 p.m. at the local library, or at the member's house whose turn it is to choose the book.)

How One Author Finds the "Write" Stuff

Todd Strasser, author of *The Wave*, the *Help! I'm Trapped In*.... series, and the book for the movie *Drive Me Crazy*, has some definite opinions about the "write" time, tools and turf that work for him.

Where do you write?
I write in a room with lots of windows so I can look outside and see the world (well, at least a backyard and some squirrels).

How do you find time for your writing?
Good question. I get frustrated by how much time I waste doing "busywork." Someone once wrote, "I love writing, it's the paperwork I can't stand." I thought they were kidding. My current schedule is to write from around 8 a.m. until somewhere between noon and 2 p.m. After that it's time for letters, e-mails, speaking arrangements, etc. Sometimes I get another writing session in during the late afternoon.

How do you observe characters, dialogue, etc.?
I'm always listening and watching. [Since I write books for teens] it helps to have two teenagers of my own.

What do you write with?
I do as much work as possible on the keyboard. My handwriting is horrible and I often cannot figure out what I wrote. So except for quick notes here and there that will soon be added to the text, I let my fingers do the talking.

Does reading help you as a writer?
Since somewhere between 75% and 90% of writing is rewriting, reading is essential. After all, isn't rewriting the process of trying to improve what you've written? How can one know how to improve one's writing without reading what others have written? Reading is probably the only way the writer can learn what "good" writing is, and then apply it to his or her own writing.

2. Agree to read that month's selected book, which is chosen by one club member, often with advice from a librarian.
3. Discuss any ground rules, like maximum number of pages a chosen book can be, or that the book must be available in paperback or obtainable from local libraries.
4. For each meeting, the person who chose that month's book should bring a few questions to discuss about the book and/or author. Take turns being the book chooser.
5. Food is optional, but a definite plus!

NOW YOU'RE GOOD TO GO!

Getting started writing means making the time, creating the space and having the tools ready. One author writes in a little white cottage in the middle of a cornfield that her husband built just for her to write in. Another writer uses the kitchen table when no one else is home and works only on Sunday afternoons. One novelist had a full-time job as an elevator operator and took her writing "snacks" on the subway to and from work every day. Like these writers, you will discover what works best for you too. Finding the "write" time, tools, and turf will help your creativity blossom and is the first step to becoming a real writer!

JOURNAL IDEAS

Cut this page out and glue it into the front of your journal for inspiration.

_____ Daily events

_____ Your daily thoughts, reactions and feelings

_____ Lists: your favorites of anything, your least favorites, Top Ten lists, current movies, CDs, singers, songs, sports stars, cool words, quotes, books… anything!

_____ Weird/interesting cut-outs: articles, photos, head-lines

_____ Random mementos: movie/concert tickets, a leaf, a flower, a note passed to you in class

_____ Sentence-starters for journal writing: This reminded me of…I wish…Speaking as so-and-so, I would say…I wonder…If that happened to me…I would change…If I could do it over again, I would…I can't imagine…What surprised me was…At first, I thought…, but then…

_____ Reviews of movies, concerts, CDs

_____ "Stream of consciousness" writing (write without even *thinking* what words are pouring out onto the page. Don't stop for five minutes. Then check out what's there. Any patterns? Anything cool?)

_____ "Spy trip" field notes

Alina Mahvish Din, age 15

Alina won second place in the Roald Dahl Essay Contest when she was just eleven years old. She was ecstatic! Inspired by this win, she submitted a short article about Ramadan (a holy Islamic holiday) to a homeschooling journal, which was also published. Most recently, she appeared in the book *Girls Who Rocked the World 2* with her thoughts on how she was going to "rock the world" by ending negative stereotypes through her writing. For her participation in the book, she had her first book signing, which she says was one of the greatest experiences of her life.

Why do you love to write?
It's easier for me to get my feelings out on paper than saying them out loud. When I finish writing something, I feel a great sense of accomplishment, and a lasting feeling of self-respect is left within me. I try to make whatever I write come from my heart, be it a book report, essay, or a journal entry.

How do you come up with topics?
When you aren't given a specific topic to write about, and you don't know what to write about, don't stress! It's often helpful to write about something you know a lot about or something you like very much. Write about your favorite movie or role model, the way your best friend makes you smile, the smell of brownies, or a new law that ought to be made. Write about a picture that puts a smile on your face, or a frown, or the best present you ever received. Think!

Get deep into your head! As Alfred Hitchcock says, "Ideas come from everywhere."

What are some cool ideas for getting started with writing?
Write a letter to the editor of a magazine telling them why you enjoyed or disliked an article they published. Send e-mail and letters to your friends and family. Join your school's newspaper staff; if it doesn't have one, start one! Create a web site dedicated to your passion. Post your opinions on stuff from abortion to Zack Hanson on the web site *Razzberry.com*. Keep a journal, and write in it whenever your heart desires. Start a scrapbook with words and pictures that describe your everyday life.

Which author has inspired and improved your own writing?
I admire the way Gail Carson Levine writes. Her books are funny, interesting, and beautiful. Publishing companies wouldn't accept her work for a *long* time, but she never gave up. She stuck with her dream and kept writing because she knew that was what she loved to do. Sometimes I feel hopeless when it comes to writing something particular, and I wonder if I'll be able to get my feelings across. When I think of Mrs. Levine, it helps to know that even an extraordinary writer like her had discouraging moments.

What final advice do you have to other young writers?
My advice to aspiring writers is to write! Write write write. Enter writing contests, send your work to publishing companies, magazines, and newspapers. If you don't feel like sharing your work with others, then just keep a book of your work for yourself. Follow your dream, whether you're a poet, playwright, lyricist, novelist, journalist, or whatever! Write in any way you feel comfortable. Save ALL of what you've written, and will write, because, believe me, you'll be glad you did! Become pen pals with your favorite writers, asking them for advice. Never give up your dream, and don't stop writing!

CHAPTER 3

Poetry, Fiction, Sci-Fi...
Exploring the Different Genres

I *t was a dark and stormy night..." No, no, no...how about, "The spaceship slowly lifted out of Mars' atmosphere..." or how about, "I was ten years old and living on the waterfront, when my countrymen decided to dump Britain's tea into the Boston Harbor and start a war..."*

The ideas swirl inside your head, but you just can't decide what kind of story to write. You thought of a great sci-fi plot in the shower this morning...but maybe there's a brilliant poet inside you dying to get out...but newspaper reporting has always seemed appealing. Agh!

There are so many directions you can go, so many different kinds of writing—called *genres*—for you to investigate. How about science fiction, or historical fiction? Or are you a mystery fan? You might prefer nonfiction, covering sports for your school paper. Have you ever considered writing a play or some poetry? Take this completely unscientific quiz to see which genre you might want to explore.

QUIZ: WHAT'S YOUR GENRE?

1. At parties I like to...
   a) talk intensely about a current event in the news to find out what other people know.
   b) people watch. It's fun to see how the "popular kids" act and figure out who is the "rebel" in the crowd. People are *so* fascinating!
   c) observe the drama between my friends—what they are saying to each other and how are they saying it.
   d) get lost in the sound of so many people talking at once. I can pick out words here and there and make a collage of them in my head. The words don't make a lot of sense, but the weird combination fascinates me.
   e) wonder if the people around me just look human, but are really alien spies!

2. My imaginary friend is...
   a) a kid detective.
   b) an encyclopedia with two legs and two arms.
   c) a cat in a hat whose name is Pat.
   d) You're kidding, right? Who needs an imaginary friend?
   e) Chewie from *Star Wars*.

3. If I got a $20 gift certificate to a bookstore, I'd race out and buy...
   a) the newest book by Stephen King. I've already read all his earlier stuff.
   b) Jewel's poetry book, *A Night Without Armor.*
   c) a copy of *Romeo and Juliet* or a book about the making of *The Matrix* movie.
   d) *Katie.com* or a biography of my favorite hero.
   e) *The Outsiders* by S.E. Hinton or *Catcher in the Rye* by J.D. Salinger.

4. My philosophy is...
   a) "Don't let the truth get in the way of a good story."
   b) "May the force be with you."
   c) "Poetry is the eloquence of truth."
   d) "All the world's a stage."
   e) "Truth is stranger than fiction."

5. At the state fair I would spend most of my time...
   a) riding the Gravitron. It feels like you're in outer space on that thing.
   b) learning about all the different animals on display.
   c) eavesdropping on kids in the Sno-Cone line.
   d) on the Ferris wheel. I love watching the colors of the sunset and feeling the wind in my hair from up there.
   e) watching the various performers onstage.

6. My favorite thing about writing is...
    a) interviewing people and asking hard questions about important issues.
    b) getting my innermost thoughts across in the fewest, most beautiful words.
    c) imagining fantastic creatures and faraway lands.
    d) creating interesting characters that feel real.
    e) imagining how people will become my characters on stage and how the audience will react to my words.

7. When I daydream in class, I...
    a) imagine myself as a reporter, traveling in a foreign country to cover a world-changing news event.
    b) create haikus from snippets of what the teacher is saying.
    c) imagine that the teacher is actually a giant man-eating insect that can disguise itself as a human during certain phases of its life.
    d) put the whole class in a movie and think up tons of exciting plot twists that could happen.
    e) think about all the stories I could write on the subject being discussed.

8. My idea of a great weekend afternoon is...
    a) visiting a local garden and writing a long poem about a just-blooming rose bush.
    b) going to a triple-header movie marathon. Who cares if it's sunny outside!
    c) sitting at a café downtown with my journal, watching people go by and live their lives, while I write it all down for story material.
    d) coming across a reporter filming a news story. Maybe she'll interview me and I can speak my mind on the issue.
    e) playing a complex fantasy game with my friends, where we each get to play different wizards...

9. My favorite game to play is...
    a) Scrabble
    b) Life
    c) Charades
    d) Trivial Pursuit
    e) Dungeons and Dragons

10. When a teacher calls on me and I don't know the answer, I...
    a) create an elaborate story that *sounds* like it might be an answer, but is mostly just my imagination.
    b) tell him that my pet dragon burned up my homework.
    c) tell him the truth: sorry, but I don't know the answer.
    d) put my hand on my forehead and sigh dramatically... my sickness act always works.
    e) tell him that all answers are debatable anyway.

Scoring:

Add up your points for each answer you circled. Check out the meaning of your total below.

1. a) 1   b) 3   c) 2   d) 5   e) 4
2. a) 4   b) 1   c) 5   d) 3   e) 2
3. a) 4   b) 5   c) 2   d) 1   e) 3
4. a) 3   b) 4   c) 5   d) 2   e) 1
5. a) 4   b) 1   c) 3   d) 5   e) 2
6. a) 1   b) 5   c) 4   d) 3   e) 2
7. a) 1   b) 5   c) 4   d) 2   e) 3
8. a) 5   b) 2   c) 3   d) 1   e) 4
9. a) 5   b) 3   c) 2   d) 1   e) 4
10. a) 3   b) 4   c) 1   d) 2   e) 5

Key to the categories:

10-17 points: You are intrigued by real life and history. Research important current events and get to know more about **journalism** and **nonfiction** writing.

18-25 points: You love drama! You'll probably enjoy **playwriting** and **screenwriting**. Get involved in your school's drama scene and keep your eyes open for local workshops for beginning screenwriters or playwrights.

26-33 points: You have a talent for observing your world and developing what you see into stories. You'd be great at writing **fiction** and **short stories**.

34-41 points: You read each Harry Potter in one sitting, think J.R.R. Tolkien is a genius, and wish Stephen King would run for president. You are a **sci-fi/fantasy/mystery** nut.

42-50 points: To you, all the world is a poem. Feed your soul and go check out a book of **poetry**.

Now that you have a tiny idea of which genres you might be interested in, here are some descriptions to whet your appetite.

FICTION

You like to watch and observe, learn about people and relationships, share your ideas, and take your readers on adventures.

Fiction writing isn't *real* life, but feels like it is. Fiction stories are completely made up, but are often based on real-life experiences that the author had, watched others have, or heard about.

Good fiction has characters you feel like you're getting to know, places that you feel like you've visited, and plot events that keep you turning the pages. Fiction writers are excellent observers and listeners, often spying on strangers, jotting notes that seem to have no meaning at the time, and saving material that helps them remember specifics of settings. They like to learn about their made-up people and settings, and enjoy reading and listening to information on their topics. Mystery, science fiction, fantasy, horror, and historical fiction are examples of some different kinds of fiction genres you may want check out.

Mystery

Think Nancy Drew and the Hardy Boys! If you like mystery, you like stories or novels with plots where you need to put together the pieces of the puzzle to figure out who killed the chauffeur.

One of the best mystery writers of all time is Agatha Christie and you'd learn a lot about how to write a suspenseful story by reading some of her books—*Murder on the Orient Express, Death on the Nile,* or *And Then There Were None* to name a few. She also wrote mystery plays, including *The Mousetrap*, which is the longest-running play in history.

More current popular mystery writers and titles to get to know include:

Potshot by Robert B. Parker

Burning Up by Caroline B. Cooney

Abducted by Mary J. Kelso

The Other Side of the Dark by Joan Lowery Nixon

Sammy Keyes and the Hotel Thief by Wendelin Van Draanen

False Memory by Dean R. Koontz

The Kidnappers: A Mystery by Wilo Davis Roberts

Science Fiction & Fantasy

These two genres have many similarities. Both have some element of the unexplained. It might be a story about a time traveler, like Susan Cooper's *The Dark is Rising* or Madeleine L'Engle's *A Wrinkle in Time*. Both types of stories can be totally made up or can include real people as characters. If you think you might want to write sci-fi or fantasy stories, get inspired by reading a few of the masters:

The Lord of the Rings by J. R. R. Tolkien

The Golden Compass by Phillip Pullman

The Lost Years of Merlin by T.A. Barron

The Book of Three by Lloyd Alexander

The Giver by Lois Lowry

The *Chronicles of Narnia* series by C.S. Lewis

The *Harry Potter* series by J.K. Rowling

Horror

When someone says "horror," who doesn't think of Stephen King? A story fits the horror genre if it gives you the heebie-jeebies, scares the bejesus out of you, keeps you up all night…you get the idea. Like sci-fi and fantasy, horror often incorporates unknown elements. But unlike those genres, horror usually takes place in the real world—the real world gone horribly wrong. Here are some scary books that should have you quaking under your covers:

Frankenstein by Mary Shelley

Dracula by Bram Stoker

The Vampire Chronicles by Anne Rice

Almost *anything* by Stephen King

In the Forests of the Night by Amelia Atwater Rhodes

Don't Look Behind You by Lois Duncan

The Babysitter by R. L. Stine

A Density of Souls by Christopher Rice

Historical Fiction

This genre is just what it sounds like: a *made up* story set in the *real* past. *Catherine, Called Birdy* by Karen Cushman is a perfect example of how to write in this genre. Other historical novels you might enjoy are:

Ruby in the Smoke by Phillip Pullman

Frenchman's Creek by Daphne du Maurier

Quake! by Joe Cottonwood

The Once and Future King by T. H. White

The True Confessions of Charlotte Doyle by Avi

Mine Eyes Have Seen by Ann Rinaldi

Lyddie by Katherine Paterson

Bud, Not Buddy by Christopher Paul Curtis

Realistic Fiction

This is a type of fiction that places emphasis on the truthful representation of the actual. That is, it deals with situations or events in a way that you might handle them in your own life. Some examples are:

Squashed by Joan Bauer

Staying Fat for Sarah Byrnes by Chris Crutcher

Strays Like Us by Richard Peck
The View From Saturday by E.L. Konigsburg
Are You There God? It's Me, Margaret by Judy Blume
Holes by Louis Sacher
To Kill a Mockingbird by Harper Lee

Short Stories

Many of the authors we've already mentioned write in more than one genre. Many novelists, for example, also write short stories. Novels and short stories are similar in that they both have a beginning, middle, and end. But short stories are different because...well, they're *short*. That is, they are often set in a smaller time period, like one afternoon, or revolve around one particular event, instead of having a long plot with many events. Short stories have to say a lot in less space—which is not as easy as it sounds. There are a million good short stories, but some of our favorite short story writers are:

John Cheever
Chris Crutcher
Cynthia Rylant
Katherine Mansfield
Peter Dickinson
Eudora Welty
Alice Munro
Gish Jen
Shirley Jackson

Poetry

Poetry is a genre to try. Lots of authors experiment with poetry when they first begin writing. Poets can still tell a story, but they tend to experiment more with images, rhyme, the way words and phrases *sound* and how they make you *feel*. Here's just a sampling of some of the fabulous poets you really should meet if you think this is your genre:

Emily Dickinson

Maya Angelou

E. E. Cummings

Robert Frost

Langston Hughes

Elizabeth Bishop

Shel Silverstein

Dr. Seuss

Plays & Screenplays

A play is written to be performed by actors on a stage in front of a live audience. A screenplay is also written for actors, but is meant to become a film or video. The more you know about how a live production works, both on and offstage, the easier it will be for you to write these genres. Getting involved in school plays or a local theater is a great way to learn, (see Chapter 10 about writing careers), but reading these famous playwrights will also help:

A Raisin in the Sun by Lorraine Hansberry

Romeo and Juliet or *A Midsummer Night's Dream* are good
    Shakespeare plays to start with.

A Streetcar Named Desire by Tennessee Williams

The Crucible by Arthur Miller

Our Town by Thornton Wilder

Pygmalion by George Bernard Shaw

How One Author Chose Her Genre

Joanna Cole is the author of the science series *The Magic Schoolbus* and many other popular books for children.

How did you decide to write about science?
I never thought that science is a boring idea, but then I always wrote books for myself. I think I have a desire to explain complicated concepts in a simple way. Even when I was in grade school and if a teacher was explaining something a kid didn't understand—my hand would shoot up and I'd say, "Ooh, ooh, let me do it!"

Do you have to do a lot of research for your books?
It takes a long time to write one of *The Magic Schoolbus* books, in terms of research. I am very meticulous about research—I do it in depth. What makes *The Magic Schoolbus* books an extra challenge, is that I have to weave a story around the science, and make it funny as well as scientific.

How do you keep up with what is going on in your field?
One thing that really helps my writing is reading. For example, I always read the science section of my newspaper first. I read a lot of nonfiction: at any given time I may be reading about astronomy, quantum physics, mathematics, or psychology—it could be anything.

Do you always write for children?
I don't know if I would put it that way. I mean I think writers write from something that is inside them. I have a sort of age level that I am attuned to and it happens to be children rather than adults. I don't think I will ever write an adult book.

Do you ever write fiction?
Yes, I have written a lot of fiction as well as nonfiction, but always for children. The best thing about being a writer, though, is that you never know what is going to come next.

NONFICTION

You love to learn new things, gather information, read and write about real things, and share knowledge and news with others.

Nonfiction writing is all true. It could be a life story (an *autobiography* or short *memoir* about your life, or a *biography* about someone else's life) or a true story about a historical event, like the search for King Tut's tomb. It could also be a fact-based opinion piece, like an essay on school dress codes, or a review of a school play or rock concert.

Nonfiction writers like reading about their subjects and getting lots of facts and juicy details to support their ideas. They do their research everywhere, often interviewing their subjects and then publishing those interviews. They visit websites, use libraries, and scope out museums when researching their ideas. There are many kinds of nonfiction writing, but *essays, journalism, historical nonfiction, biography* and *autobiography* are a few of the most common types.

Essays

You can write an essay about almost anything—your opinion on a recent event at school, your feelings about peanut butter and jelly sandwiches, or your views on something in the news. Some great essayists to check out are:

E.B. White (yup, the same guy who wrote *Stuart Little* and
   Charlotte's Web)

A Room of One's Own by Virginia Woolf

Up in the Old Hotel by Joseph Mitchell

Journalism

Journalists cover the events of everyday life in magazines, on the radio, in newspapers, and on television. If you are interested in news, join your school newspaper and start writing about school news events. But don't be afraid to think even bigger: you could offer to cover teen news for your local paper too. To find out more about journalism, here are a few helpful books:

Best Newspaper Writing, 1999 edited by Christopher Scanlan

Associated Press Broadcast News Handbook by Brad Kalbfeld

The Best American Sports Writing, 2000 edited by Dick Schaap

The Camera Never Blinks: Adventures of a TV Journalist, by Dan Rather

Crusaders, Scoundrels, Journalists: The Newseum's Most Intriguing Newspeople, by Eric Newton, editor

Fresh Ink: Behind the Scenes at a Major Metropolitan Newspaper, by David Gelsanliter

Historical Nonfiction

If you are fascinated by history, find a topic that intrigues you and start digging. Many historical nonfiction pieces start out as magazine or newspaper articles that writers wanted to expand on. Making an article into a full-length book gives an author the chance to include a lot more detail and information for the reader. Some exciting examples of this genre are:

The Perfect Storm by Sebastian Junger

In the Heart of the Sea by Nathaniel Philbrick.

The Circus Fire by Stewart O'Nan

The Essayist at Work: Profiles of Creative Nonfiction Writers, by Lee Gutkind, editor

I Have Words to Spend: Reflections of a Small-Town Editor, by Robert Corimer

Biography & Autobiography

A biography is the story of a person's life written by someone else.

An autobiography is the story of a person's life written by that person. Both of these genres can be fascinating. Here are some old classics and some newer examples of these two genres:

Galileo's Daughter by Dava Sobel (biography)

Anne Frank: The Diary of a Young Girl by Anne Frank (autobiography)

I Know Why the Caged Bird Sings by Maya Angelou (autobiography)

Exploring different genres is a first step for all writers. Don't be afraid to experiment. You may think you only like to write poetry... until you try playwriting. Or you may only enjoy writing fiction until you come across an event or a person in history that sparks your curiosity.

August Wilson is a Pulitzer Prize winning author whose plays include *Fences* and *Ma Rainey's Black Bottom*. When he first started writing, he wrote mostly poetry and didn't try playwriting until later in his career. Stewart O'Nan had always written fiction until he heard about a horrible circus fire in 1944. The more he researched the tragic event, the more he felt he had to write the story as it actually happened. *The Circus Fire* is his first work of nonfiction.

The very best way to pick your genre is to read examples of that genre, such as the books listed here. You'll soon discover which type of writing really grabs you and will have a better idea of what *you* might want to write about.

Claire Kiechel, age 13

Claire Kiechel writes poetry, fiction, nonfiction, and a variety of other types of literature. She has entered several writing contests and kept up a correspondence with a well-known author. Ever since she was little, she has wanted to be a writer.

When did you decide that you wanted to be a writer?
My mother told me that I could be whatever I wanted to be, providing I worked hard and had my heart set on something. I took this as a challenge. There were hundreds of jobs to be imagined and I could be whatever I picked. My future changed weekly. Among those on my list were a teacher, an actress, a painter, a dancer, a designer, a lion tamer, a hang glider person (is there really such a job?), a doctor, the president—it goes on forever. However, one day it dawned on me—I would be a writer. A writer was a wonderful person, chock full of ideas and stories, bursting with creative energy. A writer was a superhero according to me, for she could do anything she wanted.

Have you ever been published?
I've sent in some of my writing, poems and fantasy stories, to magazines and contests, but haven't heard back from any of them yet. I'm still hoping though. My writing was published in the school's anthology. They published one of my short stories and some letter correspondences I had with the author Lois Lowry. She wrote two of my favorite books, *The Giver* and *Gathering Blue*.

What sort of writer do you consider yourself to be?

I was always full of stories, true ones and fantasy ones. The ones I made up were a delightful mix of fiction and reality, in order to spice up my own boring life. Everywhere I looked, I saw ideas. Imagine my surprise when I realized there were different types of writers: journalists, poets, novelists, historical writers. I mused over them a while, not knowing what to choose, and finally it hit me. I didn't have to be a specific writer: a journalist in the afternoon, a novelist in the evening, a poet by dawn, and in the morning I could free write.

It was particularly annoying when adults asked the "What do you want to be when you grow up?" at a party after they were contaminated with an over-dose of champagne. It was a tiresome question, always repeated. When asked it, I would cut straight to the chase, "I want to be a writer." Some grownups would murmur encouraging words and then move on. The other kind would ask, "What kind of writer?" I would say, seeing no other way how to put it, "Every kind." I have no doubt that when I said this many would think, "Youths, they can't be every kind of writer, you must choose." I didn't mind that, people were entitled to their own opinions. The people I most dreaded were the ones who thought this same thing, but actually voiced their opinions. This always left me in despair and an incredible longing to pour ice water down their fronts, or attack them with gooey hors d'oeuvres. However, I could never bring myself to do it, which was probably a good thing.

So, if you see me on the street, and you ask me what I want to be, you know my reply. A writer. A writer who writes everything and anything I want.

A BLANK PAGE

A blank page
Waiting to be filled
Up
With Wonders.
Full of new ideas
New creations
New thoughts
Imagine the possibilities
Imagine the consequences
Imagine
So Empty
And so white.
A dream can come true
A masterpiece can be made
It can be Life
Or Death
It can be anything.
Fill the page.
Who knows?
Just wait for thoughts to
Fill it up.
Quick,
Before
It reaches
The End.

CLAIRE KIECHEL

CHAPTER 4

Choosing Your Topic: What Will You Write About?

Y ou are sitting on a train when all of a sudden a story pops into your head about a young wizard. You jot down some notes and before you know it you've plotted out seven whole books without writing even one word of the story. When you do finish the first book, you're so broke you can only afford to make two copies of it; so you send it to just two publishers. But luckily one of the publishers loves it and before you can say "Hogwarts," you are one of the most famous writers in the world!

Sound like a fantasy? Well that is exactly how J. K. Rowling got started! For some writers, nothing is worse than staring at an empty piece of paper trying to decide what to write about. Choosing your topic doesn't always come as easily as it did to the creator of Harry Potter. In the beginning, the best thing to do is to write about what's on your mind. Even if it seems to be junk, just start writing. *Later*, when you've got the creative juices flowing, you can zero in on where you want to go with your ideas, how long you want it to be, why you're writing this particular story, and where you might want to publish it. The important thing to remember at the start is *you don't have to have it all figured out to start writing*. Just start writing.

The Old Cliché—Write What You Know

You have probably already heard teachers or writers give the advice to "write what you know." That's difficult advice for many young writers, since they often think that they don't have enough life experience to write about anything! The fact is, you know a lot.

Just think about all the adult authors who write kids' books—do you think they all *really* remember what it was like to be your age? Or what it's like to be a kid now? How *can* they know? You actually know more about that topic than most adult authors do. What else do you know about?

Your journal can be a great place to find story ideas. If you've been keeping one, look over your entries and you'll start noticing words, phrases, and even patterns of topics that you can use as story-starters, article topics or poetry refrains. Check your journal for these potential topic goldmines:

- What's been on your mind lately?
- Do you have a hobby or activity that you have lots of information on and like to talk about?
- Did something happen to make you really happy recently?
- Did something happen that made you very sad?
- Do you have a story from your life that friends always ask you to tell?

Think about what you know about normal, everyday things and write about them from YOUR point of view. When you write them down and share them with others, you will discover that what you know may be quite different from what other people know—and maybe very interesting to them, as well.

When you first start writing, the most important thing is to get your ideas written down. Don't worry about things like spelling and grammar. Don't even be too concerned about the order of your paragraphs. Later you can revise and change the order of things, as well as proofread for spelling and grammar mistakes.

How One Author Decided on Her Topic

Wendelin Van Draanen is the 1999 winner for the Edgar Award for best juvenile mystery. Her book, *Sammy Keyes and the Hotel Thief*, was her first children's mystery. There are now six *Sammy Keyes* novels and two more in the works.

How did you decide to write children's mysteries?

I have always loved mysteries and in fact had written a couple of unpublished adult mysteries. I sent sample chapters of one of these to my editor, and asked if she knew anyone I might send it to. She didn't, but said if I ever wanted to try a mystery for middle-grade readers to send it to her. There was this big click in my brain and I thought yes, of course! So I tried my hand with Sammy Keyes and wrote the first four at one time.

What experiences help you to create your characters?

Until recently, I worked as a computer science teacher. Being the computer teacher, I wound up with well... let's put it this way... the popular kids don't join the computer club or the chess club. So my room became the place where the sort of outcasts would come and feel at home and I think that all comes into play when I was developing the characters in my mysteries. Watching and listening to what is around you is so important. And I remember what it was like to not be very comfortable with other kids—I guess most of us go through a phase like that. When I write I just kind of fall back on being in seventh grade again.

What do you hope readers get from your mysteries?

I hope readers can identify with Sammy to the point that they feel they can learn something from her without feeling like she is giving them a lecture. Making Sammy a believable character is just as important to me as making her a super sleuth.

And whatever you do, *don't throw anything away*. It's better to make a folder for each topic you decide to write about, then date and save everything you write about it…even if you hate it. It may feel very dramatic and satisfying to crumple up a page and toss it in the trash, but that's not a very smart thing for a writer to do.

Stephen King so hated his novel *Carrie*, the story of an unpopular girl who uses her telepathic powers to get revenge on teasing classmates, that he threw it in the garbage! Luckily, his wife rescued the story and convinced Stephen to send it to publishers. *Carrie* became his first published novel and made Stephen King rich and famous. And it almost didn't make it past the garbage can! You can use *everything* you write, even if it's only to learn what you did wrong.

TOP 10 LIST OF DO'S FOR DECIDING WHAT TO WRITE ABOUT:

1. DO write what *you* feel like writing, even if it seems terrible at the time.
2. DO try "free writing" random words and ideas that pop into your head.
3. DO re-read your journal, notes, and scribbles.
4. DO make lists of boring things you know about (who knows, they may be fascinating to other people!)
5. DO write real dialogue from your own life, but change it to suit the characters in your story.
6. DO include smells, sounds and colors…even the not-so-pretty ones.
7. DO write down your dreams every morning. There could be some great stories there.
8. DO listen to the people around you. What's bugging them? What are they talking about? Write about that.

9. DO write down single sentences. Even if you don't have a story yet, you may think up a great sentence. Write it down and save it for later. The right story for it will come.

10. DO describe your characters. Like the single sentence, a character may form in your head before the story does. No worries—just describe him or her in detail and save it for when the story comes later.

TOP 10 LIST OF DON'TS
FOR DECIDING WHAT TO WRITE ABOUT:

1. DON'T use erasers, whiteout, deleting, or scratching out.
2. DON'T crumple up pages.
3. DON'T say, "This stinks."
4. DON'T throw anything away.
5. DON'T watch TV or play video games! If you need a break, take a walk.
6. DON'T distract yourself with the phone or e-mail. (Save these until you're finished with your writing time.)
7. DON'T distract yourself by cleaning your room.
8. DON'T worry about spelling, grammar, organization or logic.
9. DON'T doubt yourself as a writer.
10. DON'T give up!

Still stumped for a topic to write about? Never fear! Just try your hand at a few of the fun writing exercises in the next chapter.

Charlie Lodge, age 13

Charlie Lodge writes humorous stories inspired by his friends and family. He hasn't been published...yet.

How do you come up with your ideas?

Let's see...most of my stories are remotely true. One of my favorite things to write about is my daily activities, such as school, television, my family, and sports events. I guess the reason I like writing about my family is that they are easy targets. I spend a lot of time with them and they aren't very normal. As for how I come up with my ideas, I like to observe people being themselves, and then take notes.

What style of writing do you most enjoy?

My favorite genre of writing is called "Creative Humor." A creative humor story is kind of like a hyperbole, meaning, I think of an event (mostly having to do with my family), exaggerate my thoughts, and write about it. Take my little brother for an example. "My little brother eats paint balls." That is a bit of a lie, but he has tried them before.

This Indian legend is a little example of Charlie's creative humor:

The Tale of Dogs

Once upon a time there lived a tribe called the Greenfeet tribe. The Greenfeet were a very peaceful tribe living in the sub-arctic region of northern Florida. Every night the Greenfeet would have amazing pow-wows (parties) with live music such as Jimi Running Fox Hendrix. Every night when the Greenfeet were having these parties, all the dogs of the village would have a huge bow-wow (dog party). The one bad thing about these dog parties was that all the dogs would have such a great time, but while doing so, all the dogs would get whipped in the face by each other's tails. So, they decided that before you could come into the party you'd have to take off your tail and leave it by the door on a hook.

Now, the Greenfeet were neighbors with the Seminoles. All the Seminoles just so happened to have their own cats and every night the cats would have their Meow-wows (wimpy cat parties). Since the dogs had such big parties, their music could be heard for miles past the village. One night the cats were enjoying their laid-back cat party and suddenly Fluffy stood up and said, "I can't take it any-more." So, all the cats sneaked up to the door of the dog party and switched all of the tails. When each dog came out of the party, he just grabbed the tail that was on his hook and wore it home. That is why whenever any dogs meet other dogs they always sniff each other's tails.

CHAPTER 5

Writing Exercises: How to Get Unstuck Fast

You're curled up in your favorite writing chair with your favorite yellow legal pad on your favorite orange clipboard and no fewer than two sharp pencils. Yes! You are ready to write, you are dying to... enter that contest/submit a story to that magazine/write your brains out! You're sure that the words will start rushing out any minute and your trusty pencil will be ready to catch them. Here they come... any minute now...you're still waiting. Agh! Nothing's happening!

Writer's Block

You've probably already heard the dreaded term "writer's block." It happens when writers just can't get their writing to go right or even put pencil to paper. One writer described it as "staring at a blank piece of paper that stares right back at me in silence." Some writers, like John Grisham, J.K. Rowling, and Stephen King, are very methodical and produce a new book every year. Other authors take much longer. But every author experiences writer's block—the feeling that your mind is as dry as the Mojave Desert! If *you* get stuck, don't worry. You're in good company. Just like any writer, you will have to figure out a way to get past it. A great way to leap past your writer's block is to try some fun writing exercises. Try one of these and you will FEEL BETTER FAST and have pages of lovely words to show for it.

TEN WRITING PROMPTS

Have you ever heard of a "stage prompt"? During a play, there is always one person with a copy of the script, who sits in front of the stage and whispers lines to actors who forget what they're supposed to say next. This is called "prompting." All an actor usually needs is the first few words of his speech and then he's off and running. A writing prompt works the same way. It gives you the start of an idea to take off from in your own writing. Here are some writing prompts that will easily help you get unstuck fast:

1. Behind-the-Scenes Fairy Tale

Write a fairy tale from a character's point of view that explains his or her personal issues (which you will invent). For example, you could become the wolf in "Three Little Pigs" who just wants the pigs to stop building on his front lawn. Or the the mouse in Cinderella who feels ridiculous all dressed up in human clothes and driving a pumpkin. Or Grumpy the Dwarf who has chronic depression that is made worse when that dumb girl invades his house.

2. Man, I Loved That...

Warm up your creative muscles by writing a review of the last movie, concert, sports game, etc. that you saw. Write not only your opinion, but also how the audience around you reacted.

3. Reality Field Trip

Take yourself on a field trip and interview someone in your town: a firefighter, gas station owner, school custodian, EMT worker, or mailman. Jot down a few simple questions ahead of time, like, "What gave you the idea to do this job?" "Was it tough at first?" "What do you like about it?" "Have you learned anything about our town as a result of your job?" "What advice would you have for young people who might want to go into your field?" Then, just *listen* and take as many notes as you can.

4. A "Secret" Conversation

Make a list of at least ten secrets, wishes, and/or problems that your friends have. Next, create two fictional characters and give each of them *one* of these secrets, wishes or problems. Finally, write a dialogue between your two characters. Write it like a script, using initials for the character's names and starting a new line each time there's a new speaker. Don't write any description or background, just write what they say to each other. Make their words express their secrets, wishes or problems.

5. Acrostic Poetry

Although *acrostic* might sound like a disease, it's actually a guaranteed cure for filling up a page with writing! An acrostic poem starts with a word, phrase or name—it could be your name, a character in a book, or even your favorite cookie.

Write the word down the left side of your page, one letter at a time on each line. This is your poem's "spine word." Then use the letter on each line as the first letter of the first word on that line, and keep writing after that word to complete the line. Don't worry about making your poem rhyme. It just needs to relate to your "spine word." Lines can run from one line to the next, so each line doesn't have to be a complete sentence. Here are a few samples. Can you spot the spine words?

Animals are irresistible
Nothing beats their furry little faces
Impossible not to love
Must be animals!
Adorable, everyone wants one…
Lost in their own dream world all day long.

—ANTONIA SOHNS, AGE 12

Powerful words written together,
Often staying in a person's heart forever
Even if they are not wanted. Poems are like
Music to the heart and food for the
Soul.

–ZOE NOVENDSTERN, AGE 13

6. Fabulous Fables

A fable is a story that usually has animal characters and a lesson at the end. Remember the story about the tortoise and the hare? That's a fable. The hare is fast, but overconfident that he will win the race. The tortoise is slow, but persistent and humble. When the tortoise wins the race, the moral is "Slow and steady wins the race."

You can write your own fable, using animals with human characteristics. Start with a wise saying (such as "Look before you leap," "A fool and his money are soon parted," etc.) and build your story from there. Consider which animals would best represent the human virtues and vices you've chosen: a fox could be sly, an owl wise, a sheep dumb, a butterfly concerned with beauty, etc.

Another way to create your own fable is to write a story about something that happened to you in real life, but replace the people with animals that have the best and worst characteristics of the real people involved. By turning a true story into an animal fable, you can say almost anything you want. Just be sure to change the names or your sister Anna may not be too happy when she reads your fable "Anna the Annoying Aardvark"!

7. Can't touch it, taste it, smell it, hear it, or see it, but...

An "abstract" concept is something you can't use your senses to perceive; you can't touch it, taste it, smell it, hear it, or see it. Anger, love, greed, envy, vanity, selfishness, thoughtfulness, and rudeness are just a few abstract concepts. Pick an abstract concept and make it come alive—make it a character with a name and an appearance. This character should totally represent the abstract concept through his other appearances, actions, and speeches. Then have your "abstract" character join a baseball team, lunch table, or trip to the mall. Tell the story from there. How does this person affect everyone around him? What kinds of trouble might he get into?

A variation on this idea is to bring a season to life. What if Summer, the new girl in school, strolled into your homeroom one wintry morning. What would happen? Or how about a land where each season lives? The season's personality and appearance could match its season—Summer might be warm and loving, while Winter is icy and distant. Just think of the interesting conflicts that could arise!

8. Memoirs-R-Us

A memoir is a story based on a memory. Think of a story from your own childhood, especially a really funny, sad or scary one. When you write it down, tell it as clearly as you can, even if you can't remember every detail. Write in the first person ("I remember...") or the third person ("Cathy woke up that morning..."). Write as much as you can, as fast as you can. Next, go back and add a few conversations and details like colors, smells, and sounds. You will be amazed at how "official" your little story sounds now—the one you've known so well that it never seemed worth writing down. Until now…

9. Odes to the Ordinary

An ode is a long, formal poem that is meant to be a serious song of praise. Odes usually praise a person, thing, or idea that is highly distinguished or admirable. Odes also have a reputation for being serious, intellectual, and…well…stuffy. That's why writing an un-stuffy ode about something completely *ordinary* can be lots of fun. Award-winning poet Pablo Neruda once wrote a wonderful poem called "Ode to My Socks." In it, he describes his socks in great detail, as well as his thoughts about the person who knitted them.

You can choose something or someone that you know very well, and write a poem or prose-poem (a poem in paragraph form that doesn't rhyme) that goes into great detail about it. You don't have to gush; just point out the traits you think deserve praise. Although it isn't necessary to rhyme, you should try to use some formal words ("thou dost"="you do" "thou art"="you are" "enwrapped"= "wrapped up", etc.) to contrast with the not-so-formal subject of your poem. Here some ode ideas to get you started:

Ode to…

1. …*My Karate Belt*
2. …*My Running Shoes*
3. …*A Math Teacher*
4. …*The Teddy Bear*
5. …*My Skateboard*
6. …*Final Exams*
7. …*My Cat*
8. …*Little Brothers*
9. … *Pajamas*
10. …*The WB Channel*

10. You've Got Mail!

Well, you *will* get mail, if you send some first! Write a letter to your favorite author or politician about an issue that's important to you. It's pretty exciting to get a letter back from the President of the United States, the U.S. Senate, Michael Crichton or Nathaniel Philbrick—and we know lots of kids who have!

Be sure to include your name and address in the top right-hand corner of the page, plus your full name and signature at the bottom of the letter. Send author letters to their publishers. You'll find the publisher's address inside the author's book, on the page across from the title page. To find addresses for government officials, check out these websites: www.whitehouse.gov or www.speakout.com.

In your letter, don't be afraid to state your true opinion, even if you didn't like part of an author's book, or you disagree with a politician's beliefs on a certain issue. But remember to always be respectful or the reader won't finish reading your letter and your efforts will be wasted.

In a letter to an author, you might write about:
- your favorite books by that author
- why you like those particular books best
- questions about the author's characters or plots
- questions about how the author got certain ideas
- why you like to write—and ask for advice!
- a thank you for writing such books and for reading your letter

In a letter to a politician, you might write:
- about an issue that concerns you
- why you are concerned about it
- how you got interested in the issue
- what you think the politician should do about it
- questions about what the politician has already done on that issue
- a thank you for considering your ideas

TEN WRITING PROPS

Each of these exercises requires a prop that can be found anywhere: a photo, a pet rock, or a good people-watching spot. This time, the prop is the key that will unlock your creativity. Follow these directions and you'll be writing fabulous stories before you know it!

1. Writing from a Photo

A photograph is a story frozen in time, just waiting for someone to release it. You can be that someone! Look through your own photo albums, magazines, or postcards. Choose a photo and climb into it, walk around in it, and imagine as many details as you can. If there are people in your photo, *become* one of them. What are you thinking? What just happened?

Write from different points of view: the third person ("It was so hot the maple leaves drooped. Maggie sat under her tree and untied her sneakers…"), the first person ("It was so hot that day the leaves on my thinking tree drooped straight down. I sat in its shade and took off my sneakers to cool down.") or both…some surprising things might surface!

2. Use an Author as a Model

Copying your favorite author isn't always "cheating." It can even be a great help for getting started with your writing. Try looking at the first few paragraphs of a favorite book. Choose three sentences and copy them, substituting new names and mostly new verbs, nouns, adjectives and adverbs. Keep the basic sentence structure the same. Here's an example from *Alice's Adventures in Wonderland*:

> "Alice was beginning to get very tired of sitting by her sister on the bank, and of having nothing to do…when suddenly a white rabbit with pink eyes ran close by her. There was nothing so *very* remark-

able in that; nor did Alice think it so *very* much out of the way to hear the Rabbit say to itself, "Oh, dear! Oh, dear! I shall be late!" But when the Rabbit actually *took a watch out of his waistcoat pocket*, and looked at it, and then hurried on, Alice started to her feet..."

And here's a new version, with names, verbs, etc. changed (the new words are in *italics*):

"*Jason* was beginning to get very *bored* of sitting by *his stepfather* on the *bench*, and of *throwing stale bread to some dirty old pigeons*... when suddenly a *black squirrel* with *blue* eyes ran *across his sneaker*. There was nothing *sooooo weird about* that; nor did *Jason* think it *sooooo strange* to hear the *squirrel* say to itself *in an angry voice*, "*Oh yeah, sure, that's just what we need!!*" But when the *squirrel* actually *pulled a cell phone out of its fanny pack, flipped it open, started to mumble into it, and scampered on, Jason jumped to his* feet." (Modeled on Lewis Carroll's *Alice's Adventures in Wonderland*)

In the first version, Lewis Carroll draws us into his fascinating story in just a few lines. The new story has some similarities, but it's clear we're in new territory— a new character and plot are being hatched. Keep going after you've written these first few sentences, using your author as a model whenever you'd like.

A NOTE ON PLAGIARISM

It's fine to create your own unique version of someone else's essay, poem or story, so long as you make sure to "acknowledge your source." After the title or at the end of your new piece, write whom you got your inspiration from: "Modeled on Lewis Carroll's *Alice's Adventures in Wonderland*" or "From headlines in the *Vineyard Gazette*, July 23, 2001."

This technique is like learning to ride a bike: at first, you need someone to hold the back of your seat, but once it helps you get going, you can do it all by yourself. Once you've gotten started, let go of the original author's plot and characters, and let your story go off on its own adventure.

3. Found Poems

Wanna write a poem but can't think of any good words or phrases? Try stealing some! This is actually legal—and expected!—when you write "Found Poetry."(Of course, you have to acknowledge your source at the end of the poem.) This technique is a lot like those "Magnetic Poetry" kits, but you use paper and scissors (or the cut-and-paste option on your computer).

The idea behind found poems is to find language that is NOT trying to be poetic, and reshape it into your own poem. Look for writing in textbooks, appliance directions, or boring newspaper articles. Once you've chosen a piece of writing to work with, copy down 30-80 words and/or phrases by hand or on your computer. Next, cut out the words and phrases and start rearranging them in front of you, keeping words you like and discarding those you don't like. Eventually you'll see your words shaping themselves into new meanings and ideas.

Your "poem" doesn't have to rhyme or have a specific rhythm. Feel free to change verb tenses, change endings to singular or plural, and change pronouns to fit he/she or they/them/it kinds of problems. You can repeat lines, words, or phrases as you see fit, and you can insert or change punctuation to help your reader understand your meaning.

Although strict found poems require that you not add *any* words, this is *your* poem after all, so allow yourself two new words. But only two. Give your found poem a title and put your name at the bottom of the poem and BE SURE TO WRITE WHERE YOU FOUND THE WORDS. Here are a few found poems written by kids:

Learning A Language

The future of Latin in the United States
Relies on this book.

Enlightened upper grades in our elementary school have
All rights reserved

Even those who recognize the wisdom
Of justification

Our own experience in school
Was bad

So we want to make it
As bad for you

Here in the most difficult
To understand Latin Book
Ever written

Have FUN
And remember

Modern Languages don't mean anything
LATIN IS LIFE.

SAM SACK, AGE 13
(from the preface to *Preparatory Latin Book I: Second
2nd edition* by *William J. Buehner & John
Ambrose. NY: Longman. 1977.*)

The Wonderful World of Plastic

We see plastic objects every day

Dishes and bowls
A toy and garden hose.

Drying or cooling
It will retain shape.

Plastic—natural
Clay, glass, and rubber

From pine trees and nitric acid
More practical than a surgeon

Returning to England in 1843
With some kind of knife.

Plastic in a toothbrush company
And in buttons and combs.

Plastics, the man-made miracle.

MARY CHARLOTTE BORGEN, AGE 13
(words were taken from *Plastics:
The Man-Made Miracle* by *Walter Buehr.*
NY: William Morrow & Co. 1967)

4. Journal Jewels

Use your journal. Okay, this tidbit of advice comes as no surprise, but this time, try using it in a new way. Read through it with a high-lighter in hand, highlighting words and phrases that are especially strong, surprising or beautiful. Make a list of these "jewels" and use a few in a poem, as the key words in the first sentence of a story, or as part of a dialogue for a character in a story.

5. Pet Rock

Rocks are like snowflakes—no two are alike. And for you, no two have the same story. Go outside and find a rock about the size of your fist. Look at it carefully, turn it over in your hands. Think about what might be inside if you were able to crack it open. Imagine you could shrink and walk on and into your rock—what would you see? Write down the details of your rock world. Describe the environment, any creatures that live there, how they survive, how they communicate. Keep going—this kind of thing can get pretty magical…for just a rock!

6. Halloween All Year

When you write about a character, you are actually putting on a mask and creating his or her voice and movements and feelings. Sometimes a real mask can get you going in directions you never considered. Look around your house, ask friends, or visit a party or costume shop and find a few interesting masks.

Put your mask on, look at yourself in the mirror, and start talking in your new *persona* (role). Write down what your character might say if talking to others. Then, write what she might say to herself—the truth about how she feels about herself and what she must do in her life. Use this character and your observations as the basis of a story.

7. Spin-off A Missing Chapter

Take a favorite book and write a chapter that the author left out. You might focus on a minor character, giving readers his point of view, or you might reveal behind-the-scenes details which you create. You could come up with a surprising new short story. In TV, this is called a "spin-off."

A variation on this idea is to write a new prologue (events that happened *before* the story begins) or epilogue (a summary of everything that happens to each character *after* the book ends) for the famous story.

8. Smell-O-Rama

The sense of smell has been proven to be the quickest path to memory. So why not take a field trip down memory lane, via the spice cabinet in your kitchen. Sit down with a few spice jars and a pen and paper, and smell the contents. Choose one and get lost in the memories or images that come to you. Write about what the smell reminds you of and soon a poem or a memoir will start magically forming as the scents waft around you.

9. Memories in the Attic

Go into your attic or hallway closet and dig out a few of your old toys. Play with some of them—bounce the pink ball, open up the *Operation* game, pull the string in the Buzz Lightyear doll. Freewrite about how you felt about the toy. Were there special rules you made up? Was it your favorite for a while? Did you get it at a birthday party? Which one?

Or *become* the toy and write in the first person using the toy's voice. Tell the reader what it's like to be the poor guy in the *Operation* game or the over-pulled Buzz Lightyear doll.

10. Write a Script Based on Someone Else's Story

Hollywood does this all the time! Take your favorite story and turn it into a play or movie. At the start of each scene, write in italics how the stage is set and the props to be used—remember, the audience won't hear these words, but the director will use them to set the stage and guide the actors.

Write the name of each character in capital letters before his/her lines. Write the lines spoken out loud in regular print. Include directions to actors in parentheses before or after their lines.

Follow the story closely, and feel free to use words from the story's dialogue. You will have to change most of the descriptions into actions or dialogue spoken by the actors. Some of the story can be changed into stage directions, which you will write in italics. This way, the reader can tell the difference between words that the actors say out loud and the actions that they do or the sights the audience sees.

This is a great exercise to do and then act out with friends. But don't forget to always acknowledge your source—the title and author.

When You're Not Totally Broken Down, Just a Bit Stalled...

There will be times when you won't need to launch into a whole writing exercise. Perhaps you have a great idea already but at the moment your mind seems to be a blank wall. Those words you just had in your mind seem to have flown out the window. Try these mini-writer's block cures.

Walk away.

When you feel you have nothing left to write, take a break. Go shoot some hoops or take a long walk with the dog. When you're not thinking about your writing, you may find that next paragraph suddenly appears in your head. One writer busts her writer's block in the car. She puts on her favorite CD and just relaxes. Sooner or later she gets unstuck, pulls over and jots down her thoughts.

Start in the middle...or at the end.

Sometimes you may have a great idea, but not a great first sentence.

Don't worry. There's no rule that says you have to start at the beginning. You could write your ending first, or start somewhere in the middle. You could start your story by writing a really interesting scene or character instead of the beginning. Whatever works for you is just fine.

Keep souvenirs.

If you are writing a story, it can help to keep something on your desk or in your pocket that inspires you: a photograph or some object that reminds you of one of your characters.

Use scissors. (Just don't run with them!)

What if you like what you've written but it doesn't seem to be in the right order? Well, there's always that wonderful computer tool called "cut-and-paste." But sometimes it helps to physically move your paragraphs around too. Try this: print out your writing with enough space between paragraphs that you can actually cut them up. After cutting them apart, take your pieces and spread them out on the floor or a large kitchen table. Then move your text around and hear how it sounds. After you've rearranged, you can go back to the computer and copy the rearrangements.

And Don't Forget to Recycle: Save Everything!

Did you write anything with the prompts or props in this chapter? If you did, good for you! You probably have some great stories or poems already started. No matter what you think of them, save all of your first attempts. When you re-read your writing later, chances are you'll be saying something like, *Hey—did I write this? Not too shabby!* Your writing will seem fresh, and unique—and maybe even good enough to send to publishers. And, we'll tell you how to do just that in the coming chapters!

Milana Bogorodskaya, age 12

Milana Bogorodskaya is an immigrant from Russia who left her home country at a young age. She has written many poems and fiction stories, as well as nonfiction stories about her own interesting experiences.

How did you start writing stories?
I was born in St. Petersburg, Russia. When I was seven, we moved to America, where everyone spoke English. Even though my parents taught me English in Russia, I still couldn't communicate. Kids tried to get to know me, but I couldn't understand them, so I practically had no friends. Then I met my next-door neighbor. She was a year older than I was, but we got along great. We made up many stories together, and one of our special ones was "Vampires." I am really good at starting a story, but I never seem to finish it. I found out that I love to read and write. There's a poet that I've been reading lately, Pushkin. He is from Russia like I am and I think his poetry is very good.

Has your writing evolved since then?
My mom was trying to pass really hard exams, so every Saturday and Sunday when I didn't have any plans with my friends, I would go to the library and stay there with my mom until it closed. The librarians even knew my name. After four years of living in Peabody, MA I found out that my mom found a residency in Louisville, KY. I was devastated. I had finally found true friends, and now I was moving again. How could this be happening?

So, at the end of June we drove all the way to Kentucky. When I got to Kentucky, I didn't have any friends, so instead of hanging out, I wrote stories about kids who had the same situation as mine. I also wrote in my journal, and that really helped me, because I was very depressed. Recently I realized that I could get published, so right now I am working on a story. I've even entered a poetry contest, but I didn't win. I'm going to keep trying though, and soon I'll win and my poetry will be published.

Do you have any advice for other young writers?
Don't be afraid to get criticism, because that's what improves your story. There's a kid I share my stories with and he gives me good advice. He told me that I should use more detail in my stories and so now I do. This is great advice, because I know that I enjoy reading stories with lots of detail. I've also been writing in my English class at school. Our teacher always gives me helpful criticism with my writing. We have a portfolio in the classroom for our writing and our parents and friends and relatives come one day to read and give advice on our writing.

RUSSIA

A winter is cold
But it is fun
Climb the snow mountains
Dance around the Christmas tree
Eat chocolate sweets
Falling snow is beautiful
Greatest of all the greatest things
High mountains are covered
with snow
It's finally spring
Jumping into snow slush
Kind of wet
Lilies starting to spread
Morning is like a veil of fog

Now comes summer
Out of school you go
Picking berries, and mushrooms in
the woods
Quiet birds begin to sing
Raspberries sweet upon the vine
Sunshine in your eyes
Through the fields you run
Under the leaves you hide
Violin music fills the air
Waves splash against the shore
You are invited to my birthday
Zip through the leaves that fall
from trees

MILANA BOGORODSKAYA

CHAPTER 6

The Process:
Writing and Rewriting

Okay, you're glued to your keyboard and the words are coming out fast and furious! You've decided your genre. You even have a great topic in mind. In fact, you have a great character, a great beginning and a knock-'em-dead ending. This book should be finished by dinnertime, no problem! Well, just as soon as you figure out what goes between the beginning and the end, that is!

How long does it take to write a masterpiece? A day? A weekend? Ten years? Yes, yes, and yes. There's no telling how long it will take to write a really great book. Author Margaret Wise Brown wrote *Goodnight Moon* in a weekend and it became one of the best-selling children's books ever written. On the other hand, some writers spend their whole life writing *just one book*.

There's no right way to write a book, and there's no time limit either. Every writer discovers a process that works best for him or her and each writer's process is unique. Yours will be too. But, as you begin writing your masterpiece, keep in mind:

1. You will rewrite it later. No matter how fast they wrote it or how great it is, all writers polish their work.

2. You may get stuck. Every writer hits writer's block sometimes. But don't worry... the tricks in Chapter 5 will help you get unstuck.

3. It's okay to start all over again. Sometimes an idea just doesn't pan out and it's better to move on to something new and fresh. That doesn't mean you won't come back to your old idea again. Don't throw it out! Stick it in one of your files to look at later. You never know—there may be something there after all.

The Writing Process

When inspiration strikes, you should begin writing immediately. Getting your initial thoughts recorded while the creative juices are flowing is critical. Otherwise, you may forget that amazing flash of brilliance. In fact, you probably will...that's why it's called a "flash." Don't worry about anything besides putting your thoughts on paper: let the words flow no matter if your words are misspelled or your punctuation is wrong. You can go back and fix these details later.

What's a "First Draft"?

The term "first draft" sounds pretty serious, but it's not. It's just your first attempt at writing a story. Your first draft may be the framework of a story that you will fill in later. Or it could be a complete work that you won't change much during your rewriting process. Your first draft can be handwritten on a pad of paper, typed on a computer, or even spoken into a tape recorder—whatever works best for you to get your thoughts out. Go for it. One writer wrote the first chapter of her book on a bunch of napkins on an airplane!

How many drafts will I do?

That's up to you, and again there is no right answer. Your first draft is for getting your thoughts down. Later drafts are for polishing your story—adding details, reworking scenes, making dialogue more realistic, etc. Once you've written your first draft, put it away for a while—a day, a week…however long it takes until you can read it as if it were the first time you were reading it. You want to be able to come back and read it with fresh eyes. This will help you see where your writing needs work. Many writers also find it helpful to have a friend, teacher or writer's group read their first drafts and give them comments on what is good and what could be improved (more on this in the next chapter).

Most writers will do at least two drafts before they feel their writing is finished. When you go back and re-read your first draft, you may find a scene that just doesn't work or a character that doesn't quite fit in. Don't be afraid to cut material that doesn't work. It will make your writing stronger. But don't throw it away—that cut material may be the beginning of another story!

In writing this chapter of our book, for example, we started by writing the first draft in pencil on a big yellow legal pad. Next, we read it over and made notes and changes in the margin before typing it up. Then we put the first draft away for a week. When we came back to it, we made more improvements and fixed the grammar and spelling mistakes (we love spell-check!). After two or three drafts, we finally had a final draft of Chapter 6 ready to send to our publisher.

GOOD WRITING STRUCTURE—THE BASICS

We certainly don't want to tell you exactly how to write—that's the fun, creative part. But if you notice that your story doesn't really grab the reader and you want to add some zip to it, take a look at these basics of story structure for some ideas:

CONFLICT

If you're writing a story, script, opinion piece, or essay, chances are that your writing needs a conflict—or a problem—to keep your reader's interest. A conflict is a struggle between two opposing forces. In a story, the conflict is usually between the main character (also called the *protagonist*) versus something *external* or *internal*:

External conflict: the main character is in conflict with something concrete, like another character (the Wicked Witch of the West, Darth Vader, annoying little sister, bully, etc.) or a force of nature (a tornado, the perfect storm, quicksand, etc.).

Internal conflict: the main character is struggling against something abstract, like a parent's expectations, peer pressure, society's morals, or even his own conscience. An internal conflict is a struggle within a character's heart or mind. Here are some good examples of internal conflicts your character might have:

- Whether or not to steal the leather jacket he/she can't afford to buy but really, really wants.
- Being the first boy/girl to join the school dance team/football team.
- Going out with someone his/her parents hate.

CHARACTERS

Your story should have a *protagonist* (the main character), and an *antagonist* (the person, thing, or idea that causes the central conflict). You might also have minor characters that come in and out of your story as it progresses, and who might even supply some minor conflicts. It helps to write down your characters' traits. You can even draw sketches of them to keep all their characteristics in mind as you write. As your story progresses and goes through revisions, you'll want to change those sketches too.

Here's a great form for remembering the important traits of your characters. Fill out a Character Sketch for each character in your story.

Character Sketch (Fill in the blanks)

name _____ (check out books for naming babies—they have cool names and their meanings)

gender _____

height _____

age _____

hair color _____

eye color _____

race _____

religion _____

fashion style _____

loves to _____

hates to _____

hopes to _____

favorite saying or word _____

pet peeve _____

Once you have filled in a Character Sketch list for each person in your story, you can use these descriptions as details in your writing. Each trait can become a source of conflict in your story, as well. You don't have to describe your characters directly to the reader to get their traits across. In fact, it's usually more interesting if your readers learn about a character in more subtle, indirect ways—by how other characters react to her, what they say about her, or by what the character says and does. Here's an example of how you might describe a character directly or indirectly:

Description: *Dorothy was a thoughtful girl who yearned for a more interesting life filled with adventure, friendship, and love.*

How others react: *The Cowardly Lion, the Tin Woodsman, and the Scarecrow left everything and followed Dorothy, knowing she might lead them to what they wanted and needed.*

What others say: *"Don't worry," said the Tin Woodsman to the Cowardly Lion, "Dorothy won't hurt you."*

What the character says or does: *"Why, you poor thing," Dorothy said. "You are all rusty. I'll help you. Where's the oil can?"*

SETTING

The setting is the time and place in which your story is set. Go back and add as many details about your setting as you can. You might think your reader sees the same things you see in your head, but add the details anyway. Stimulate the senses: put in smells, tastes, sounds, feelings, and sights. Be sure that your reader has a clear sense of your story's setting from the beginning or she will feel lost while reading it.

One young writer went back and added a fall setting to her story late in her writing process. By describing the red and yellow colors of the season, she was able to emphasize the fiery dangers lurking in her story's central conflict. Writers often use their setting as a metaphor or symbol for their conflict or their characters' feelings. For example, you may wish to have a storm brewing outside your main character's window to symbolize her struggle over what to do next and her feeling that trouble is coming.

Setting can be a great source of drama. Have you ever felt mysterious while walking through a fog? Or peaceful while basking in the sunshine? Your setting descriptions can be effective parallels to your character's feelings.

As with your characters, creating a Setting Sketch can help you better describe your setting.

Setting Sketch (Fill in the blank)
year _____
time of day _____
location _____
sights/scenes _____
weather _____
smells _____
noises/sounds _____
physical feelings _____ (scratchy sand beneath toes, biting wind against cheeks, stifling heat in the waiting room, etc.)

PLOT

Unless you want your reader to be left unsatisfied, your should make sure that your story has a beginning, middle and an end. And those three elements should be *balanced*. Too often, a writer starts out with lots of details and description at the beginning of his story, but by the end he seems tired of writing and the whole story gets solved too quickly to be interesting or believable.

The Beginning

Often called the *exposition*, this is the part that gets the reader familiar with the basic characters, setting, and conflicts. You want to include an event that shows the reader what the conflict is (also called the *inciting incident*). Can you figure out the inciting incident in *The Wizard of Oz*?

> *Dorothy is bored on her farm in Kansas, has an unpleasant encounter with the witch-like librarian, and then a tornado whisks her and her house to the Land of Oz.*

The Middle

This is usually the longest part of the story, and has three parts to it:

1. The build-up—This is the part of your story where you create tension (also called the *rising action*) and hook your readers into reading more. After the inciting incident, include some events that develop the conflict.

> *Dorothy lands in Oz, sets off on her journey, meets and befriends the Scarecrow, Tin Woodsman, and Cowardly Lion, battles the Wicked Witch, etc.*

2. The climax or turning point—At this point, something *big* happens that brings the central conflict out into the open and gets other characters involved in it. Your reader should really know what the problem is, and wonder how it will be solved.

One Author's Writing Process

Chris Crutcher is the author of numerous books for young readers including *Ironman, Staying Fat for Sarah Byrnes, Stotan!,* and *Chinese Handcuffs.*

How do you start writing your books?
The best I can say is I think of a story and then I tell it. I get started by looking at the heart of the story, what it is about, and begin with some action.

How much rewriting do you do?
I do a tremendous amount of rewriting. Because I start with just the seeds of an idea, it means that as things happen in later chapters, I have to go back to earlier chapters to match them up. I also write down "everything," and not everything belongs in the story. I do a LOT of rewriting.

Do you ever have a hard time giving up a great idea that doesn't quite fit a story?
Not anymore. I usually know I'll be able to use it somewhere else. The hard part is realizing that it doesn't belong.

How do you get over writer's block?
I go away from the story and do something physical and let my mind loose.

Dorothy and her friends discover that the Wizard is a fake and may not be able to grant their wishes after all.

3. Falling action—this is a fancy term for everything that happens after your climax. Your falling action should show that the conflict is winding down. Don't skimp on this part and don't rush it—your readers deserve to know just how things get worked through.

Dorothy and the Wizard work out solutions for each of her friends' problems. Then the Wizard tells Dorothy how she can get home to Kansas.

The End

This is also called a *conclusion* or *resolution*. At the end, you need to settle the conflict. Be sure your characters say and do believable things here. Go back to your character sketches and look for clues that may help you create things they do or say to solve the problems in realistic and believable ways. You might also set your ending in the same place as your beginning—this helps your reader feel that the story has come full circle.

> Dorothy clicks her red shoes together, chanting "There's no place like home. There's no place like home," and is back in the original setting—her farm in Kansas. Her family and friends, who closely resemble her friends from Oz, surround her. Their comments and loving concern prove to her that there is no place like home.

STEPS IN THE WRITING PROCESS

The writing process is a series of steps that the writer goes through before his writing is considered "finished." Writers sometimes stop writing in the middle of the process, put it away, then pull it out later to start writing again. Some writers finish an entire piece over the weekend. No matter how long it takes, most writers go through the following steps for each writing piece.

1. Pre-write or free-write. This can mean writing in your journal or using writing prompts and exercises.
2. Write a first draft.
3. Revise the first draft.
4. Get responses and comments from others.
5. Revise it again, based on reader responses.
6. Check the piece for spelling and grammar mistakes.

7. Decide where the piece might be published and get submission guidelines. Sometimes this is the *first* step in the writing process (we'll talk more about this in Chapter 8).

8. Finalize the piece, making sure it fulfills the publisher's guidelines. Make a copy to keep for yourself.

9. Submit your writing to a publisher.

10. Wait for their answer…and wait…and wait…

TIME TO *GO PUBLIC!*

Phew! You're finally at the point where you feel your story, poem or play is just right. Guess what? You're still not done. Now it's time to share it with the world! Let others whose opinions you value read it. Although not everyone will like what you have written, that's okay. You can't please everyone, right? But other people's opinions can be very helpful, as you will see in the next chapter. Letting people read your writing, then listening to their opinions can be hard, but *it will make you a better writer*. And whether you take their advice or not is totally up to you. You are the final judge of your writing.

So, whether you're ready to have others read your writing or are ready to submit it to publishers, read on!

Holly Tederington, age 10

Holly Tederington says that she wrote her first poem when she was three (with *some* help from her father). In first grade her teacher and principal thought a book she had written was so impressive that they sent her to the Young Author's Conference in Toledo, Ohio. Soon after, Holly set her sites at becoming a widely recognized author.

What do you love most about writing?
Writing fiction is fun for me because I can exaggerate and defy the odds.

Have there been any monumental experiences in your writing process?
I kept reading books that turned out boring. I thought, "What if there was a book with never a dull moment?" I decided that book would be written by me! After a few pages, I ran out of ideas, but as I went on with my normal day ideas were constantly popping into my head. Problems from your normal life often fit into your writing.

Do you have any more tips on overcoming writer's block?
Get some circulation going! I usually read a book. Sometimes, the easiest way to start at the beginning is not to start at the beginning. Try beginning at the end and working backwards.

Which author has given you inspiration?
What made me mostly want to become an author was reading. My favorite

books are the Redwall Series by Brian Jacques. I soon discovered that I wanted to write books like he does. In my writing now the planets talk and the owls wear glasses, because I got the ideas for including animals as characters from the Redwall series. Animals in these books live in a place called Redwall Abby set in a fictional country.

What is your dream as a writer?
My goal for my writing career is to become a famous published author. It probably won't happen anytime soon, but I get closer and closer with every page.

This is an excerpt of Holly's writing:

Everyone watched and listened.
  The bush moved!
  They all froze, afraid of what would come out.
  The bush moved again!
  Something was coming out, but everyone was so scared, they felt paralyzed. They tried to run, but couldn't. Their feet felt cemented to the ground. Whatever was in the bush was about to leap out. They could almost count down.
3. . . 2. . . 1. . .
  Everyone prepared for the worst. No one was ready for what came out, though. It was. . .Squeaker the Chipmunk! Squeaker leaped right out of the bush causing Rodney, Prickles, Iris, and Cashew to scream.
  "What?" asked Squeaker. "What?"
  Rodney breathed a sigh of relief knowing very well that there was nothing to be afraid of.

CHAPTER 7

You've Written Your Masterpiece... Now What? Let Them Read It!

You finally found a way to end your story with something besides "…and they lived happily ever after." Your setting is full of great descriptions and you added some new dialogue. You even ran it through spell-check. Nothing left to do now but print it out and … oh no! Horror of horrors. You have to let a real human being actually READ your writing!

Actually, you don't *have* to let anyone read your writing. Sometimes it's fun to write something just for yourself, something that no one else will see. But there's a difference between being a writer and being a *published* writer. You are a writer as soon as you start writing. But to be a published writer, you will have to let someone else read and judge your writing. And it *can* be pretty scary to show your writing to someone else.

So, now's the time to make your decision. You've spent a lot of time and effort writing something and you feel pretty good about it. Are you ready to show it to someone you trust? Getting a reader's opinion is incredibly valuable to you as a writer. Once your piece is out there—submitted to a publisher, contest, whatever—it's done. It's too late to find out what messages readers will understand from your writing, and whether they will discover your true meaning. Asking someone to read and respond to your writing is a great opportunity to receive valuable feedback *before* you finalize your piece.

What is A Reader?

A "reader" is someone who will read and respond to your writing—that is, readers will give you their opinions on what they think is good and bad about what you've written. Unfortunately, very few people know how to respond to writing beyond checking the spelling and grammar. Don't you just hate it when you want someone's opinion, but all they do is point out your misspelled words? That's what spell-check is for. But you can bet that most readers will assume spell-checking is all you want them to do, unless you tell them otherwise. Readers who give you feedback about your plot, your characters, your word choices, etc, are much more helpful to your writing.

HOW TO FIND A GOOD READER

How do you choose someone to read your work? There are two kinds of readers you should consider asking:

1. Readers who represent the people who will actually want to read your piece (otherwise known as your *intended audience*). If you're writing a kid's book, have a kid read it. If you're writing about a teen girl, have a teen girl read it. See if it's believable and enjoyable to them.

2. Readers whose opinions on writing you value. Both types of readers are extremely valuable to you as a writer, and each can offer you different insights. We're sure you can think of a

WRITING GROUPS

Joining a writing group can be a fantastic way to grow as a writer. A writing group is just a group of writers who share and comment on each other's writing on a regular basis. You can find a writing group to join by asking teachers and librarians in your area. You can even start your own group! Just find a few friends who like to write and...

Writing Group Checklist

1. set up a regular meeting date and time (for example, on Tuesdays at 3:30 every week, or every other week, or the first week of each month)
2. set up a regular location (schools, libraries, and local bookstores are often very willing to give you space if you ask, or rotate at each other's homes)
3. assign a leader (or set up a list to take turns) who will:
    *   bring one fun writing prompt
    *   keep the group on task
    *   watch the time.
4. snacks—a must! They are a great way to stay energized. Take turns being in charge of this crucial task.
5. use the same meeting agenda each week (see below).

Meeting Agenda

Here's what to do during the meeting time:

1. freewrite (write non-stop on any topic) for 10 minutes. Don't worry about spelling, grammar, or complete sentences.
2. do a read-around of all or part of each free-write, with no comments (laughing, however, is allowed!)
3. present a writing prompt and write silently for 10 minutes.
4. do another read-around of parts or wholes, with comments on what was strong or stood out.
5. End the meeting by reading pieces that members brought to share with the group. These are usually pieces that were started in previous sessions, but have been revised and finalized. It's nice if the author prints out enough copies for each member.

few good people who will read your writing and give you their responses: teachers, parents, grandparents, aunts, uncles, the local librarian, and of course, your friends. But don't ask *too* many people to be your readers. You know the saying, "Too many cooks can spoil the soup"? Well, that goes for your writing as well: too many readers can spoil your story. If you get too many opinions, you will have a hard time deciding whom to listen to. Find one or two people you trust and ask them first. Save everyone else for your next stories.

WHAT TO ASK YOUR READER

Believe it or not, you will probably have to coach your reader a bit in order to get the helpful responses you're looking for. Before you ask people to read your writing and give you their opinions, know what you want from them. Fill them in on the parts you struggled with and are still worried about. Tell them what you'd like them to look for and what types of suggestions you'd like. Here are some things to say and questions to ask your readers before and after they read your piece:

1. I think I am (still in the early stages/almost finished) writing this piece.

2. I'd really love your ideas on how to improve the beginning of the story (or the setting, or a particular character, or whatever you need).

3. Which words, phrases, characters, or plot events, etc. stand out to you or seem particularly strong?

4. Which seem particularly weak?

5. Were there any gaps in the plot or a character that needs more description?

6. How did the writing make you feel? Did it remind you of anything?

7. Is there anything you would change about the piece?

FEAR!

Okay, we all have it, especially the fear of criticism or rejection. In fact, most writers have an especially hard time with it. Writing can be a very personal experience, and showing your personal thoughts to someone else is not easy. It might help to keep in mind that a reader's opinion is just that—one opinion. There are probably other opinions out there too. It's *your* writing and *you* are the one who decides whether to change it or not. If one reader's opinion doesn't work for you, get another one. Remember, your reader is just trying to help, not rip your heart out.

You and your reader should understand that there is no right or wrong way of viewing a piece of writing, just what the reader understood when she read it. Later, you will decide whether you communicated your idea well or whether you need to make any of the suggested changes to help other readers get your point.

WHAT TO DO WITH READER COMMENTS

1. Remember that this is your writing and any decisions about changes are up to you. Reader comments—you can take 'em or leave 'em, but no matter what, you should think about them.

2. Remember that *you* asked for their comments and your readers are only trying to help. Always say thank you. They took

What One Author Does After the First Draft

Katie Tarbox is a teen author who wrote the novel *Katie.com: My Story*, a true tale about her experience meeting an online friend. After six months of e-mails, fourteen-year-old Katie discovered that the "friend" she thought was her own age was really a forty-year-old man—and he was interested in more than friendship from Katie.

What is your writing process?
I just write everything down at first, like vomit on the page. Then I go back and rework. I have found that since I have been exercising a lot more lately, I think about my writing while I am on the treadmill and then come back and write. Sometimes even before the shower. Writing is something that must be practiced and maintained on a daily basis, so I try to write every day.

How much rewriting do you do?
I do a lot of rewriting, because I like to reflect on what I have written. I like to think about how I can reword it, change it around, form it into the best possible prose I can. For me, it's the most important part of writing.

Whom do you let read your writing before it's finished?
My editor of course has to read it, but first I like to bounce it off my family and friends. I am constantly asking them for their input.

Did you ever feel like giving up while writing your book?
No, I never felt like giving up because I felt so passionately about what I was doing. I am a tenacious person to begin with, so giving up is not in my personality.

time out of their busy lives to read and think about your writing. Even if you disagree with their opinions, you should be grateful for their help.

3. Jot down notes about what they said. Did they seem confused? Did they ask questions? Can you give them answers by adding to or clarifying your writing? Did they seem interested in a particular point or character and want to know more about it? Think about where you can add, delete, rearrange, or reword to make sure your future readers get just what you want them to get from your writing.

4. On the computer, make a whole new copy of your story and put the word "revised" in the title. Keep your original just as it is. Work on the revised copy and don't touch your original. Save it for later.

5. Start revising. Clarify, add, delete, rearrange—experiment. You can always go back to the original if you're not happy with the revisions.

6. Put the writing away after you have revised it. Come back in a day or two and read it again with fresh eyes. You'll probably be encouraged by your progress and might even be tempted to revise it some more! Don't worry—go ahead and make it even better. We won't tell!

CONGRATULATIONS!

You've finished writing something, you've revised it (probably more than once), and you've even shown it to a few people and received feedback from readers. Give yourself a big pat on the back and treat yourself to some chocolate chip cookie dough ice cream—a time-honored tradition among writers! Now it's time to move on to bigger and better things—it's time to share your writing with the world!

Young Author Profile

Valieshia C. Wells, age 15

Valieshia C. Wells has immersed herself in writing. Nineteen stories and two screenplays later, she is well on her way to becoming a writer. She found that writing articles for her newspaper and local magazines was a good place to start.

How did your love of writing begin?

I started to write when I was in the 6th grade in Juneau, Alaska. A lot of things were going on at the time between my mother and father and I was caught in the middle. One day I had my pen and paper near me and I was daydreaming. Abruptly I began to write. And suddenly I had the urge to write more. I said to myself, I like to write, and it feels good to have something to let all the pain and frustration out.

What do you enjoy most about the writing process?

Every time I feel like crying, I write. Every time I need a friend, I write. Every time I need to feel loved, I write. Writing has become a soul-saver for me. It has lifted my spirits, given me independence, and raised my self-esteem 100%. My writings are an outlook on what I am and who I am. To me writing is my world, and my world is writing.

What type of writing have you been working on lately?

I'm currently working on a mystery novel and a horror novel. I just got this idea into my head one day and started writing about a month ago. Now I'm on page 250, but can't quite decide on the finishing details. My school has been trying to put together a literary magazine and I am collecting poetry from other students to include in it. We're looking for a publisher right now.

Do you have any favorite books or movies?
My favorite director is Steven Spielberg and my favorite movie is *Titanic*. My favorite piece of writing is "The Raven" by Edgar Allen Poe.

How are your screenplays coming along?
Well, I've written two screenplays start to finish, "I Can Be Your Queen" and "Brown Eyed Girl." The first one is about two royal families and the conflicts and discoveries of their children who have immigrated to the United States. The second describes one girl's experiences in moving to a new town across the country and having to make new friends at high school. I'd love to actually put these scripts onto film, but I can't find enough people willing to act it out. I know how to use a camera and have had experience producing commercials for a school project in eighth grade. My biggest goal right now is to turn one of my screenplays into a book and get it published.

CHAPTER 8

How to Get Published: Creating a Proposal

Loud
and
Clear

The alarm goes off and you bury your head deeper under the covers...until you remember TODAY IS THE DAY! You are finally going to show the world your writing. Three drafts and three critiques later, you know you have a masterpiece. But how do you get the rest of the world to read your writing?

So, you've got that final piece of writing in perfect shape, your readers are responding to it the way you want them to, and you're ready to send it out...but where to? A big part of being a writer is (dare we say it?) doing your HOMEWORK! Different magazines and book publishers look for different kinds of writing. You want to make sure that whom you send your *manuscript* to is the right person to read it. This doesn't guarantee that he'll publish it, but at least you'll know you've got your foot stuck in the right door.

Step 1: Figure Out Your "Market"

The first step in getting published is figuring out what is the best market for your material. And no, we don't mean go to the grocery store! "Market" is a term magazines and book publishers use to describe the kinds of people who will buy a particular book. For example, if you read only nonfiction history books, you probably won't be *in the market* for a romance novel! Most editors say the worst sin new writers make is sending them writing that isn't appropriate for the market they publish for. That may sound complicated, but it's not. If you have a great nonfiction piece, don't send it to a publishing house that only does fiction books! *That* sounds pretty simple, doesn't it? But you wouldn't believe how many writers don't think about where they send their manuscripts—they just throw 'em out there and hope for the best!

So, how do you find the right market for your writing? Well, you already know which genre your work falls into (you did read Chapter 3, right?). Next, decide whom you wrote it for—who's your *intended audience*? Is it for young kids? Is it for teenagers? Is it for all ages? Once you've got those two things figured out, it's time to start searching for the magazine or book publisher who publishes that genre for that market.

Your librarian or English teacher are great people to go to for information and help. You'll find many companies out there that actually specialize in publishing the writing of young people like you! Check out our list in the back of this book. A good place to begin your search is at your local library, with a book called *The Literary Marketplace* (or "the LMP" for those in the know). This huge book, which gets updated every year, weighs about fifteen pounds and includes the names and addresses of most publishers in the world plus tons of magazines and contests. Each listing describes the genres that company publishes and the markets they publish for. Here's a sample listing from the LMP, describing the publisher of this book:

A LMP LISTING

Beyond Words Publishing, Inc.
20827 N.W. Cornell Rd., Suite 500, Hillsboro, OR
  97124-9808
SAN: 666-4210
Tel: 503-531-8700 Toll Free Tel: 800-284-9673
  Fax: 503- 531-8773
E-mail: info@beyondword.com
Web Site: www.beyondword.com
Key Personnel
Publr & Intl Rts: Richard Cohn E-mail:
  richard@beyondword.com
Pres & Ed-in-Chief: Cynthia Black E-mail:
  cynthia@beyondword.com
Man Ed: Julie Steigerwaldt E-mail:
  julie@beyondword.com
Children's Dir: Michelle Roehm E-mail:
  michelle@beyondword.com
Mktg Dir & Lib Sales Dir: Sylvia Hayse E-mail:
  sylvia@beyondword.com
Founded: 1983
ISBN Prefix(es): 0-941831; 1-885223; 1-582700
Number of titles printed annually: 20 Print; 2
  Audio
Total Titles: 125 Print; 3 Audio
Online services available through the World Wide
  Web.
Imprints: The Earthsong Collection; Kids Books
  By Kids
Distributed by Publishers Group West
Foreign Rights Rep(s): Deep Books of London
  (England); Jay Books (New Zealand)

Another great way to figure out your market is to go to your local bookstore to find books that you think are similar to your masterpiece. Make a list of the companies who publish these books (you'll find the information in the front of the book on the copyright page, usually the first or second page in the book). If you think a magazine is better for your writing, do the same thing in the magazine racks. Most magazine and book publishers also have websites you can visit, which will tell you more about the books and articles they do. Sometimes you can even request a catalogue be sent to you, right over the Internet—for free. If you find some book publishers and magazines that have already published your type of writing, they're the most likely to publish that type of writing again, right? You've figured out that your markets match. Way to go!

Step 2: Get the Guidelines

Okay, so you've found a bunch of magazines and book publishers that you think might be interested in your work, based on the kinds of material they publish. Narrow down your choices to five to fifteen places—you don't want to go bankrupt on stamps and you need to be able to keep track of where you send everything. Before you send anything to anyone, however, GET THEIR WRITER'S GUIDELINES! Writer's guidelines are a checklist of what a magazine or book publisher is looking for, and how they like to receive *submissions*. Some companies will want to see your whole manuscript, others just want to see an outline and maybe a short writing sample. All the companies will send you their writer's guidelines for free— all you have to do is call them and ask or check their websites (writer's guidelines are often posted there too). This step is incredibly important—if you send a magazine or book publisher your writing, but don't follow their writer's guidelines, they're more likely to reject your work. And that's the last thing you want, right?

SAMPLE GUIDELINES

Guidelines for Tricycle Press

All Tricycle Press submissions are considered on an individual basis, although a personalized response is not always possible due to the volume of submissions we receive. Please note that we do accept simultaneous submissions.

* DO NOT SEND ORIGINALS OR YOUR ONLY COPY OF ANYTHING. We are not liable for artwork or manuscript submissions.
* Send an appropriate SASE.
* Allow 8 to 20 weeks for a reply.
* Be sure your work is appropriate for us. Familiarize yourself with our list by going to bookstores or libraries. We encourage you to request our catalogue by mailing a 9 x 12 envelope with $1.02 in postage (no checks or cash, please).
* Correspondence regarding status of manuscripts should be done by mail—no phone calls, please.
* Please do not send queries.

Activity Books: Ages 3 to 12. One-third to one-half of the manuscript is usually sufficient. Submit a table of contents or outline. Illustration ideas are often helpful but not necessary.

Novels for Young Readers: Ages 8 to 12. If it is in chapters, please submit two to three sample chapters; otherwise one-third to one-half of the manuscript is usually sufficient. Also submit a table of contents or outline.

Picture Books: Ages 3 and up. Complete story is necessary; illustration ideas are often helpful but not necessary.

Real Life Books: (books about and for kids to help them understand themselves and their world; includes parenting books): Ages 3 to 13. If it is in chapters, please submit two to three sample chapters; otherwise one-third to one-half of the manuscript is usually sufficient. Also submit a table of contents or outline.

We encourage you to look at the following book: Children's Writer's Market.

Thank you for your attention, and good luck!
The Editors
Tricycle Press
P.O Box 7123, Berkeley, CA 94707

Step 3: Manuscript or Query?

When you get your writer's guidelines, they will tell you to send either a completed *manuscript* or a *query*. Manuscript? Query? What the heck are those? Again, strange words, but simple meanings. A manuscript is what magazines and book publishers call your piece of writing. If they tell you to send your manuscript, that means you should send your entire poem, story, book, whatever, for them to read.

A query is more of a teaser. If they tell you to send a query or query letter, that means they want you to send them just *a description* of what you've written. They don't want to read your actual writing unless they're interested in the idea. If they like the idea in your query, then they'll ask you to send the entire manuscript later.

Make sure you send exactly what they ask for. If a book publisher wants to see a query, don't send a manuscript. If a magazine wants to see a whole manuscript, don't send a partial one. One of the first keys to success on the road to publishing is that you've got to follow the rules! You don't want to give these companies a stupid reason to reject your writing. You want them to at least read it and be impressed that you're smart enough to follow their directions.

Step 4: Creating Your "Proposal"

After you get your guidelines and know what you're supposed to send, it's time to create a *proposal*. A proposal is a package deal that includes four very important things: 1) a *cover letter*, 2) your *manuscript* (or query), 3) some *market research*, and 4) a *SASE*.

Your Cover Letter

Make sure your cover letter is no more than ONE PAGE long! A great cover letter should do three things. First, it should grab an editor's attention. Make your cover letter short, interesting and funny! Editors get pretty bored reading dozens of identical cover letters every day. Make yours stand out from the rest. Make that editor wake up and pay attention to you.

Second, your cover letter needs to summarize what your manuscript or article is about—briefly! This is not the place to write pages and pages about what they'll going to soon read anyway. Keep it short and sweet—two to three sentences.

And third, your cover letter should include a little bit of information about you: any writing awards or contests you may have already won, work you do for your school newspaper or literary magazine, what inspired you to write this particular piece, and even your hobbies or why you want to be a writer.

The following is an example of a great cover letter written by a teen author. The author, Daryl Bernstein wrote this letter on his own—without help from his parents or teachers. In fact, his parents didn't even know he was submitting to publishers until his book was accepted!

SAMPLE QUERY LETTER

Beyond Words Publishing, Inc.
20827 N.W. Cornell Rd., Suite 500
Hillsboro, Oregon 97124-9808

Dear Beyond Words Editorial Board:

I am a fifteen-year-old honors student in Scottsdale, Arizona. I have been running my own businesses for the past five years with great success, and I am an avid *Wall Street Journal* reader.

I am interested in publishing my book, *Better than a Lemonade Stand: Small Business Ideas for Kids*. The book explains to kids of all ages how to go into small business and succeed with little or no investment or parent help.

The potential market seems excellent. The book is of interest to any kid who wants to make a buck. I have thoroughly researched the books on the subject, and have found only two in print. Both are written by adults and use language for adults rather than kids. The books are also weak on organization and provide little or no explanation of how to really start a business.

While doing my market research, I came across one of your "For Kids by Kids" books. I found the book interesting, and I felt that your publishing style will certainly appeal to kids. Although I am also considering large publishing houses, I would like to deal first with a company that has past experience in publishing for and by kids.

I am enclosing a few sample pages from my book, which is currently in progress. Please write if you are interested in publishing the book.
I look forward to your response.

Sincerely,

Daryl Bernstein

Your Manuscript

Once you are 100% *sure* that the manuscript you are sending follows the requirements of the magazine or book publisher, double-check that your manuscript...

1.   ...has **a title page** with your name, address, phone number, and e-mail address in the upper right hand corner; a word count and page count on the upper left hand corner; and the title of your manuscript in the center of the page, with your name underneath.

      You can certainly get creative with your proposal, but keep in mind that colored paper and wacky typefaces are often more annoying than interesting. A standard-size (8 1/2 x 11) white paper, with one-inch margins all around, and a basic, readable font like Times is your best bet. Let the creativity of your words and ideas grab their attention, not some hot pink paper or gothic script.

2.   ...has your name and the title of your work at the top of EVERY page, just in case your title page gets lost somewhere. It's also good to put page numbers on the pages, in case a clumsy editor drops your stuff and pages go flying.

3.   ...is double-spaced. Editors like to have room to write their comments in the margins.

Your Market Research

Here's where you can really get a head start on your competition. Very few writers include market research in their proposal, but publishers love it! What you want to include is one page, titled "Market

Betsy Kohn is Editor of Guideposts for Teens

What advice would you give kids who want to write?

Just DO it and have fun. Don't expect to get paid at first. Write a profile of somebody interesting and see if you can get it published in your local newspaper. Write a poem for your high school magazine. Write captions for the yearbook. And read everything you can get your hands on—fiction, nonfiction, magazines, newspapers, *TV Guide*, the phone book—whatever! Do crossword puzzles.

Mostly, just pay attention to everything around you. Listen to how different people talk, and notice how people and places look, sound, smell. Be a detail person. A story will come alive if you can communicate the FEEL of a person, put someone right in his or her shoes—and you can only do that if you pay attention to things.

What do you do as an editor?

I sniff out good stories—get them written, and reshape them until they're fit to print. I glean story ideas from newspapers, other magazines, TV, etc.—as well as from writers who pitch them to me. I have to make sure that each issue has a good balance—a variety of stories that will appeal to all of our readers. This takes a lot of organization and planning.

Once I decide to go for a story, I assign it to a writer and work with him or her on revising—until it's close enough for me to dig in. Then I rework sections, making everything flow together.

Teamwork is really important in editing—I brainstorm with my boss and other editors about themes, writing techniques, etc., and I ask our readers (teens!) to give feedback from time to time. I also work with the art department, coming up with ideas about how the story will be presented graphically. Then there's proofreading, making up headlines, paperwork (like paying the authors), and (gasp!) in my spare time, I write my editor's column!

Research," which describes the audience or market for your book, any similar competing books, and any unusual places a publisher could sell your book (besides bookstores).

Since you've already done your homework, you should know who your market is. For submissions to magazines *and* book publishers, you should write something like, "Any guy between the ages of 12 and 16 should love my book/article on...," or "children ages 4 to 8 and their grandparents, parents, and teachers will all enjoy reading my book/story."

The second step on your Market Research page is just for book publishers—if you're only submitting to magazines, just skip it. After listing who you think will want to buy your book, list a few other books out there that are similar to yours and *how yours is different and better* (if no other books like yours have ever been published, good for you! Tell them that.) Maybe you wrote a book about great after-school snacks for teens. You could mention that other book you saw that had after school recipes for kids, but point out that it was written for very young children while yours is written for teens. And the other after-school snack book that *is* written for teens is really boring and lame, but yours is hip and cool. This is where you tell the editor why your book is *so* important.

And last, brainstorm some ideas about where a publisher could sell your book, besides in bookstores (again, skip this step for magazines). Your after-school snack book could be sold in kitchen stores, grocery stores, and even high schools! Think outside the box...be creative. Make the publisher see how many people will love to buy your book.

Market research is the first thing book publishers do when they get a manuscript they are interested in. And even magazine editors will find your information helpful. By sending them market research with your manuscript, you're doing their homework for them! And who doesn't love it when someone does their homework for them?

Your SASE

Ahhhh! Another weird word! Fear not... S.A.S.E. just stands for Self-Addressed Stamped Envelope. What it means is this: if you want your manuscript sent back to you (just in case, for some unthinkable reason, the magazine or book publisher decides *not* to publish it), your proposal package needs to include an envelope with your name, address, and postage on it.

Your SASE *must* have enough postage on it to get back to you. If not, kiss your manuscript goodbye—companies not only won't return it to you (if they did that for everyone, they'd go broke pretty quickly!), they'll get annoyed that you didn't read their rules. Make sure that you weigh your manuscript at the post office on a letter scale so you know how much postage you need to mail it out and put on your SASE.

Step 5: Keeping Track

Once you start sending out your work, you need to keep track of where it's gone! Every time you send out a proposal, write down:

1. What you sent.
2. Whom you sent it to.
3. The date you mailed it.
4. How much it cost to mail.
5. How long the magazine or book publisher is supposed to take to respond (this is listed in their writer's guidelines).
6. The date you get a response, plus any comments they give you.

Some writers keep a box with index cards to keep track of everything; others keep a list on their computer. Whatever works for you is fine, but do something. It's better to keep track as you go along than to try to remember later.

Step 6: The Waiting

Now's the hard part—waiting. Keep track of when your chosen magazines and book publishers are *supposed* to respond to your proposal. If they say it takes them eight to twelve months to respond, then don't start freaking out after six months! If eight months go by and you haven't heard anything, it's perfectly fine for you to give them a call, send a letter, e-mail or postcard to find out what's up. *Do not* call before their time is up!

Since it can take months to get a response to your proposal, and since you'll probably go crazy waiting, this is a good time to KEEP WRITING! Cut out the following checklist and stick it somewhere you can easily find it as you start sending out proposals (like on your bulletin board or the side of your computer) and don't forget to check it every time you send something out...even if you *think* you remember all the steps. Better safe than sorry!

Checklist for Proposals:

My proposal includes:
1. A cover letter
2. My manuscript:
    - has a title page including my name, address, phone number.
    - is double-spaced, has one-inch margins, plain paper and fonts.
    - has been checked for spelling and grammar mistakes.
    - has my name and the manuscript title on each page.
3. Market research
4. A SASE

If this all seems like a lot of work, well you're right, it is, but look at the bright side—you have written something you want the rest of the world to see. You are definitely on your way. Just remember when you were still wondering what you would write about! You may not see your work published next month, or even next year, but if you stay with it, you will make it as a writer.

Dallas Nicole Woodburn, age 13

Dallas decided to write a book, publish it, and sell it when she was in fifth grade. That year, she asked for a small grant from the Parents and Advocates of Gifted Education to print her book *There's A Huge Pimple On My Nose: A Collection Of Short Stories And Poems*. She was granted fifty dollars, and printed the 42-page book up at Kinko's herself. After passing out some fliers to fellow students, she found herself back at Kinko's printing out more copies of her book, because it was so popular and in such high demand that she had run out of copies to sell. The money she made from this book went towards paying back the grant. She says that not only was she able to pay the grant back for future students' projects, but she paid back the grant two times over.

Have there been any reviews done on your book?
There's A Huge Pimple On My Nose has been reviewed in the *LA Times* newspaper and *Girls' Life* magazine. And you won't believe this—I still can't—but I also received a letter from "Dear Abby" saying how much she enjoyed my book! I'm a little overwhelmed—no, A LOT overwhelmed—but it feels nice. I feel like I've really accomplished something. I am so grateful that everyone is so appreciative of my talent and hard work! It's unreal!

How did you feel about the surprising success of your first published book?
I can't believe all the attention I'm getting from my book! I talked at a school in Thousand Oaks about my book and about writing in general. I told them to not worry about writer's block, just to write what they feel, for that is something I have always done and is one of the reasons why I like writing so much.

I am free to say whatever I want, whatever I feel. I also told the fifth- and sixth-graders to not be afraid of setting their stories and poems aside for weeks or even months, and to come back and rewrite, rewrite, edit, edit...that's the best way to improve your writing. I also encouraged them to read, read, read, because that helps broaden you vocabulary and make you a better writer.

Have you had any special attention or experiences as a result of your literary successes?

The man in charge of the Santa Barbara Book Fair invited me to come be a featured author at it! In addition, he named the day "Dallas Woodburn Day" in honor of me winning an essay contest! My friends think it's so cool! So do I! I was again privileged enough to be a featured author at the Author's Fair at Cal Lutheran and got to give a talk and sell my book there. It was a lot of fun, and has really gotten me excited about writing another book!

Have you gained any insight into the writing process of young people, like yourself, that you'd like to share?

I often reflect on everything that has brought me where I am and the steps I took to get here. It's hard to believe that this whole big project started out with one little fifty-dollar grant. That one small step snowballed into a giant leap, and now, five hundred copies and two book fairs later, here I am. My confidence has snowballed, too.

I feel I have grown so much. Before I published my book, I used to be shy, and the thought of giving a speech in front of people scared me. Now, I have gained so much confidence from giving book talks that I enjoy speaking before audiences!

If I've gotten one thing out of this experience, it's that anything is possible, if you put your mind to it. Anything. I want to be a female Mark Twain, or the next Emily Dickinson or Sharon Creech. No wait, make that the *first* Dallas Nicole Woodburn.

CHAPTER 9

Getting Published:
What To Do If They Say No...
What To Do If They Say Yes!

S cenario #1: *You rush home from school, yank open the mailbox, and...yes! It's a letter from a publisher! Your hands shake as you open it. Your eyes have trouble focusing, and then you read that killer first sentence: "Thank you for your recent submission, however it does not fit our editorial needs at this time." Bummer. That's your twelfth rejection letter! You're starting to wonder if you've got what it takes to be a writer after all.*

WHAT TO DO WHEN THEY SAY NO

Be prepared: it is very, very likely that you will get rejected a few times before you get your first piece of writing published. This is part of being a writer. Welcome to the club. Every writer gets rejected at some point. But remember, it's not YOU that is getting rejected. If a magazine or book publisher says "no" to your proposal, that only means that your writing wasn't *suitable* for that particular company at that particular time. It doesn't necessarily mean your writing is no good—it could mean that an editor just published a book similar to yours, or that the magazine has decided to go with a different kind of material for the next few issues.

Whatever the reason, if you have sent your very best work, don't be discouraged. Rejection doesn't mean you don't have talent. If you are serious about getting your work published and are willing to do the homework, you *will* succeed. Keep sending out those proposals and keep on writing. Your day will come.

Also keep in mind that just because your story didn't work for an editor in November, it may be just what she's looking for in May. Don't be afraid to re-submit your proposal, if you are really convinced it's right for that magazine or book publisher. You may even be sending your story to a totally new editor who has never seen it before. Times change…and so do editors and their interests. So, don't give up.

WHAT TO DO WHEN THEY SAY YES

Scenario #2: The phone rings and you pick it up. It's an editor from Teen *magazine asking, "Is Megan there?" Your fingers go numb and it takes all your strength to keep from dropping the phone. Your knees start to buckle and your voice shakes as you squeal, "Yes, I'm Megan!" As the editor says, "We'd like to use the manuscript you sent us." You practically faint! It's your dream come true.*

Don't drop the phone and *do* sit down! This could be your reality. When your writing is finally accepted for publication, it will surely be one of the most exciting moments of your life.

Besides staying cool, calm and collected, what are you supposed to do if your dreams come true and they say "yes"? If you work hard and do get something accepted for publication, there are a few things you should know about the business side of writing.

When a magazine or book publisher agrees to publish your

work, the first thing that will happen is that you will receive a contract to sign. You may say, "It's all Greek to me," when you see that first contract, but the good news is that *legalese* (the *legal* language contracts are written in) will get easier for you to understand the more you get published.

CONTRACTS AND GETTING PAID

The rules are different with magazines and books, so we'll describe both.

Magazine Contracts

Magazines will pay you one time for using your writing. But not all magazines (and especially those that feature writing for kids) pay for writing in *dollars and cents*. Instead they may send you some free copies of the issue in which your article, story or poem appears. Or they might give you a year's subscription to the magazine.

BEWARE!

A vanity press is a company that agrees to publish your book for you, but *you* have to pay *them*, instead of the other way around. There are vanity presses out there that will even send you flattering letters or e-mails about your writing and invite you to have your writing in their next anthology of "outstanding young writers." The book may actually get published, but it will cost you a "small fee."

While you may be interested in this kind of publishing, make sure you know exactly what your fee will be and what that pays for *before* you agree to anything. Never sign a vanity press contract without getting experienced advice first. Some of these publishers are wonderful, others are not.

There also plenty of websites that will post your writing. Some of these work like vanity presses: you pay us, we post your writing. Again, that's not necessarily a bad thing, but be careful and read the fine print before you send them any money. And no matter what, it is best *not* to give your real name, address, school, or telephone number over the Internet.

If a magazine does pay you money for your writing, you will either get paid "on publication" or "on acceptance." Getting paid "on publication" means you'll get paid when your writing appears in the magazine. If your writing is accepted in March and the magazine plans to print your writing in the December issue, you'll get paid in December. Getting paid "on acceptance" is exactly what it sounds like—you get paid when the magazine agrees to buy your work. This kind of payment information should be in the writer's guidelines that you sent away for. (You did that, right?)

Take a look at this contract from one publishing company. It's fairly simple—not too much legal mumbo jumbo!

SAMPLE CONTRACT

Author's Agreement

I, (author's name) of (address), for and in consideration of the sum of (amount $____), and other good and valuable consideration hereby sell, transfer, assign, and convey to (name of publisher) a corporation located at (publisher address), all my right, title, and interest in the work, (name of article) for the (month/year) issue, including but not limited to the right to copyright and publish and otherwise use the property in any way that said (company name) in its sole judgment shall determine.

I hereby warrant and represent that I am the sole copyright owner and proprietor of the work and that the work is not in the public domain, will not infringe or violate any copyright, trademark or personal or proprietary rights of any person or entity and will not contain any material which is defamatory, libelous, obscene or otherwise in violation of the law. I also warrant and represent that I have full power and authority to enter into this Agreement. I shall indemnify and hold harmless (company name) from any and all costs and expenses (including reasonable attorney's fees) arising from any claims, suits, judgements or settlements arising from a breach or alleged breach of my obligations, representations and warranties herein. The foregoing representations, warranties and indemnities shall survive any termination of this Agreement.

I have executed this assignment at_____ on the ____day of ____, 2001.

Signature_____
Social Security Number_____

One Author's First Publishing Experience

Shannon Lanier is the author of *Jefferson's Children: The Story of One American Family*. Her book is about the descendents of Thomas Jefferson and Sally Hemings, of which Shannon is one.

How did you feel when the publisher first told you they'd accepted your book?
Let me just say that I ran up and down the hall of my grandmother's house, yelling "Thank you, Jesus." To talk and dream about doing something like publishing a book is one thing, but to actually have the opportunity to do so is a reality that could change your world. Some time after receiving the book approval I decided to breathe and think about the enormous responsibility before me.

How did you feel when you first saw a real copy of your book?
"WOW!" was just about the only word I could think of when I saw the first copy of my baby. It was literally like being pregnant for a year and a half, and when the book was completed and printed, it was like a child was born. It was so exciting to see my name on the cover of a book and the words that I wrote set in stone. Then I saw the book in a bookstore and it really became a reality.

What's the best thing about being a writer?
The best thing about being a author is having the opportunity to inspire, motivate, and feed people's souls through the words that will forever be set in stone.

Book Contracts

Book contracts are usually lots longer than magazine contracts. If you receive a book contract, you should definitely go over it with someone who knows something about contracts and legalese (lawyers are good for this) and have them explain it all to you. Always make sure you completely understand what you are signing. Each book publisher has different payment arrangements, just like magazines. For example, some publishers pay a "flat fee," which means they pay you just once like magazines. But most book publishers pay what are called "royalties."

Royalties (hey, you get to be the king or queen here!) are what the publisher pays you in exchange for you letting them publish your writing. A royalty is a percentage of the cover price for every book the publisher sells. That percentage can vary anywhere from 2% to 20% and will be listed in your contract. So, if a publisher charged $10 for your book and you got a 10% royalty, you would get $1 for each book they sold. Got it? When you get to the royalty section of the contract, get out that calculator.

Royalty checks are usually paid a few times a year, and continue as long as your book keeps selling. Sometimes a publisher will pay you what is called an "advance." An advance is a payment the publisher makes to you *before* your book is in the stores. It's not extra money, just part of your royalties that they pay you up front. If a publisher gives you a $1,000 advance, they will deduct that from your later royalty payments. Getting an advance means that a publisher is pretty confident that your book is going to sell well. Stephen King gets huge advances because everything he writes is almost guaranteed to sell millions of copies. First-time authors, on the other hand, usually don't get paid advances. And some smaller publishers never pay advances because they operate on smaller budgets.

KNOW YOUR RIGHTS

Magazines

Magazine guidelines will tell you what kind of *rights* they are buying when you agree to let them publish your work. Rights? What are *rights*? If you write something, you are legally the owner of that material—you own the *rights* to it. When a magazine buys your work, it usually asks to "buy all rights." That means that you, the author, are selling your rights to the material—you no longer own what you have written. In other words, if you sell "all rights" to one of your stories to *Teen* magazine, don't even think of trying to re-sell it to *Cosmo Girl!* That's illegal!

Don't worry too much about selling "all rights." That's what most first-time authors do when they're starting out. As you get published more and develop a name for yourself as an author, you will be in a better position to ask for more rights. Sometimes a magazine only wants "first serial rights," or "one-time rights," which means they only want the right to publish your work once, and then all rights are returned to you. With that kind of deal, you may be able to sell the same story to a different magazine or book publisher later.

Even if you sell "all rights" to a magazine, if you contact them after the piece has been published and ask for your rights back, often they'll agree. When you're starting out as a writer, getting those first few pieces published is the most important thing. Editors are more impressed if you've been published before—they're more likely to read your proposal more carefully. So, in the beginning, don't worry so much about how much you're going to get paid and what rights you can keep. You can haggle about all that when you're a famous writer.

Books

Book contracts also specify which kinds of rights they want to buy from you, and what kind of royalty (if any) you'll be paid for each. The same rules apply as for magazines: be sure to understand what you're selling and make sure you feel like you're getting a fair deal. Again, it's best to have a lawyer or knowledgeable adult go over the rights section of the contract with you.

WORKING WITH AN EDITOR

Once your work has been accepted and your contract is signed, an editor will begin working with you on your manuscript. Yes, even after all your careful writing and rewriting, chances are that your work will be edited again before it goes to print. *Everyone* gets edited, even famous writers, and a good editor usually makes your work even better. But working with editors can be a fun experience and should improve your writing—that's their job, after all.

Good editors help you fine-tune your ideas and words even more than you already have. And good authors are open to suggestions and excited to make their writing the best it can be. Editors and writers are like the two wheels on a bike—they work better together than alone! To give you an idea of just what an editor does, here is a "before and after editing" paragraph from this very book. Better, right? We thought so too!

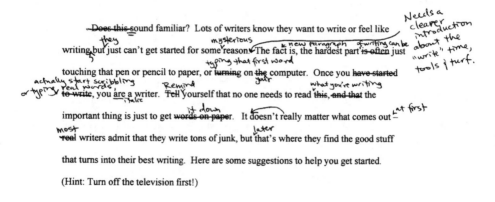

THIS IS YOUR LAST CHANCE

Once you and your editor have a final manuscript completed, you should get a final copy to review one last time. Not all publishers, especially the big ones, remember to do this. So, make sure to ask your editor for last review before it goes off to the printer. This is *not* the time for you to rewrite whole pages that you have new ideas for—it's too late for that! It's also *not* the time to worry about grammar mistakes. Point any out that you happen to notice, but a professional proofreader should catch those.

This *is* the time for you to make sure you are happy with the final edits that have been made to your book, and to make sure they haven't changed any facts in a way that would make them untrue or inaccurate. Read your copy over carefully, then send it back to the editor with any changes you find, marked in ink.

AND MORE WAITING

After your last review of the book, it's time to be patient—it's tough but necessary. There is no average when it comes to how much time passes between when your work is accepted and when you finally see it in print, but a year is not unusual, even for a magazine article. For a book, it can sometimes take several years to see the final product! Believe us, it is worth the wait! Just don't start running to your mailbox as soon as you've sent off your final corrections.

THE GRAND FINALE: YOUR FIRST BOOK SIGNING

After all your work writing and editing, and after all your patient waiting, your book will finally get published and show up in bookstores. Pretty exciting! But even more exciting is when you get to do your first book signings and interviews. This is called *publicity*. You may be nervous about this aspect of being a writer, and that's totally normal. But remember, publicity helps sell your book (which means more royalties for you!) and lets you meet the people who are reading your work: your fans! Not only do you get to see your name in print, you may even make it onto *The Today Show* (or at least get an interview in your local paper!). And what a great feeling to have a total stranger say to you, "I just *loved* your book. You're such a fabulous writer. Can you autograph my copy, please?"

We talked in this chapter about what happens if you get a magazine article or a book published, but the reality is that if you decide you wanna be a writer, you will probably write lots of different things. You will write a million cover letters, that's for sure. But it's worth it. No matter how many times your writing is published, every time you see the finished product you feel just as excited as the first time. Seeing your words in print never gets old!

And just as you can write many different kinds of writing, you can also try many different kinds of writing careers. You may start out writing novels, then move on to writing a screenplay when Hollywood decides to turn your bestseller into a movie. Or you may work as an ace reporter covering news in Europe, or as a sports writer for ESPN. There are tons of exciting writing careers just waiting for you!

Matthew (Mattie) J.T. Stepanek, age 11

Mattie wrote his first poem at the early age of three! He has now written over a thousand poems, a series of books called *Heartsongs,* and does public speaking at conferences and seminars. Born with a rare form of muscular dystrophy called mitochondrial myopathy, Mattie has to use extra oxygen and a power wheelchair every day. This year he was chosen to be the Maryland State Goodwill Ambassador for the Muscular Dystrophy Association. In 2000, a hand-bound collection of his poems was presented to the Library of Congress in Washington, DC and placed in the Children's Literature section of the national library. Mattie's poems have also been published on <u>myhero.com</u> along with renowned poets like Maya Angelou, Langston Hughes, and Helen Keller. Currently, Mattie is working on a philosophy book called *The Tao of Heartsongs.*

What kind of writer are you?
Mostly I write things that combine what I feel in my heart and my spirit with what I know in my head. I guess you could call much of what I write my "philosophy" on life. A lot of my work is poetry, but I also write short stories and essays on many different topics, and I always keep a journal. Some of my poems and stories are funny or silly. Some of them are about difficult or sad things, like when my brother died, or what it's like living with a disability, or how it felt to go through a divorce. Sometimes I write because a marvelous idea pops into my head and it becomes a story. I make an outline of chapters, then I just go and write and write and write. Other times, I might feel emotion-

ally down about something, or excited, or angry, or confused, or thankful. Whatever my feeling is, it helps to write about how it is affecting me.

What advice do you have for other kid writers?

If you are having a difficult time coming up with something to write about, start by describing something in an unusual way. For example, look outside, and describe a tree, without mentioning words like green, brown, branches, or leaves. Describe how it makes you feel or think. Describe what it sounds like. Describe how it smells. Describe a memory that it makes you think about. You can describe people, places, objects, all kinds of things. Use all of your senses, especially the ones that you wouldn't typically associate with what you are describing. The grammar and spelling and spacing can all come later. The most important thing is to get your unique ideas out. Use a tape recorder and then transcribe it, or dictate your thoughts to someone else if the actual mechanics of writing are difficult or tiresome. But get your ideas and thoughts and feelings into words, and capture them. . .for yourself and for others.

Do you ever get writer's block? If so, what helps you get through it?

Like most people, I do get writer's block. Sometimes I think it's because I have too much on my mind at certain times, or because I am trying too hard to write about a certain topic. When this happens, I slow down, and spend more time just writing in my journal. I might just describe a thought, or a smell, or list my favorite activities or television shows. When I relax and just begin writing about what I see, hear, feel, or think, the words begin to come easily. Then, I can go back, and take one of my journal entries and create a poem, essay, or short story based on what I wrote.

What is your favorite thing about writing?

My favorite things about writing are that I get to use my imagination and that I am able to share my philosophy and "Heartsongs" with other people. I always enjoy writing. No matter how I am feeling, writing makes me feel better. It helps me calm down when I am upset, it helps me give thanks and celebrate when I am happy, and it helps me organize my creativity when I have a good idea.

Here are two selections
from Mattie's extensive poetry
collection:

About Wishing

Some people think that
Wishing is childish.
But, wishing is
For everybody.
Wishing can help the
Old feel young, and
Wishing can help the
Young grow into the
Wisdom of age.
Wishing is not
Prayer or magic,
But, somewhere in between.
Like prayer and magic,
Wishing brings optimism,
And wishing brings hope.
And like prayer and magic,
Wishing brings new ideas,
And sometimes,
The touch of new life.
And that, is essential
For our future.

MATTIE J.T. STEPANEK

Angel-Wings

This Morning,
I smelled something very good.
Perhaps,
It was a rainbow.
Or maybe,
It was a dinosaur smile.
Or even,
A seashell.
I am not sure
What rainbows
Or dinosaur smiles
Or seashells
Smell like.
But I'm sure they smell wonderful.
Wonderful and special
Like the smell of
Angel-Wings.
But also,
I'm sure they smell
A little sad,
Because we can't really smell
A rainbow,
Or a dinosaur smile,
Or a seashell,
Or especially,
We can't really smell
The wonderful smell
Of Angel-Wings.

MATTIE J.T. STEPANEK

CHAPTER 10

Writing as a Career:
You Mean I Can Get Paid for That?

You just finished your article on the World Series for *Sports Illustrated, and now you have to dash over to the library to read a passage from your new book,* Another Perfect Storm, *to a group of young would-be writers. Then you have to start writing a column for* Seventeen, *profiling that hot new band. And somewhere in there you must find time to start working on that new mystery you have been carrying around in your head.*

If you decide that you wanna be a writer and earn a living at it, be prepared…your parents' first reactions may include at least one of the following worries:

- You, their precious child, will wind up starving in a garret (garret is the fancy word people use for an artist's room in the attic).

- You will become famous and weird like Ernest Hemingway and go on dangerous adventures and keep lots of six-toed cats.

- You will become even flakier and more out of it than you already are.

- You will start wearing a black beret, spending your nights at smoky poetry readings, and snapping your fingers instead of clapping.

- You will write embarrassing things about your family and friends!

A good way to keep your parents calm and on your side is to tell them that you are already taking this writing thing seriously. In fact, you're even researching how to be a successful writer by reading this book! Go ahead and ask your parents for help every now and then—get their story ideas, comments on your writing, proofreading help, and advice on any contracts you get. This is a double whammy: it gets them involved and excited about your writing career, and also gives you free help.

If you have discovered that writing is your passion, you're in luck because there are more cool and exciting writing careers than you can count. But how can you find out which ones you'd like best?

HOW TO LEARN MORE ABOUT WRITING CAREERS

1. Don't be shy about talking to a teacher or librarian about being a writer. Good teachers live to help kids in real ways. Tell them how you've become interested in writing and ask if they can help you find good writing contests or publishing opportunities. You could also ask them to help you choose your best piece to send out.

2. If your school has a newspaper or a literary magazine, get involved.

3. Write to your local newspaper and ask if they accept *freelance* writing—stories written by people who aren't on their newspaper staff. You may be surprised at the answers you get.

4. If you are interested in writing for TV, cable TV is a good place to learn about it. Many cable companies provide opportunities for kids to get involved in working at a real TV station: you can learn how to run cameras, editing equipment, and even how to write the shows. Check with your school about local cable TV stations and whether or not they accept student interns.

5. Do an internship at a book publishing company, a magazine or a newspaper. Check your phone book or ask a teacher about companies in your area, then call and ask if they would be interested in having a student intern. Be sure to tell them how hardworking and passionate about writing you are. This is a great way to see behind-the-scenes of getting published.

6. If you want to write plays or movies, volunteer at a local theater. Even if you're not into acting, there are plenty of other theater jobs that will help you learn how to write for the stage (or the big screen).

7. Read biographies of real writers to learn what their lives are/were like and how they got started. Get inspired!

8. Write to your favorite author, or call a local writer, and ask for their advice. Two young writers we know wrote letters to the author

Nathaniel Philbrick and got hand-written letters back from him all about how he researched his book, *In the Heart of the Sea*. Most authors really enjoy talking with young people about writing. After all, they had to start out once too. But it may take them a while to get back to you, so be patient and don't get discouraged.

9. Go to writing conferences. You can find some of these listed in market directories mentioned in the chapter on resources. Also, your teacher may be able to tell you about conferences specifically for young authors or visit the website for the Society of Children's Book Writers and Illustrators (SCBWI) at www.scbwi.com.

10. Start your own writing group. You can work with one person or a few and your group members don't necessarily need to be local— you can meet regularly through the Internet.

REAL WRITERS TALK ABOUT THEIR CAREERS

Screenwriter

I think screenwriting is the most fun kind of writing to do. You get to imagine a movie in your head and write it down. It's mostly action and talking without much description. And when they shoot the film, it's even more fun to see the movie from your imagination, become a real movie that everyone can see. —Cynthia Whitcomb is a screenwriter and has won the Christopher Award for her screenplay *When You Remember Me*.

Poet

I like writing poetry because things occur to me while doing it, things that wouldn't have occurred to me doing something else. Poetry is con-densed language, and just like condensed orange juice right out of the can (before the water is added) is a stronger version of the juice you drink, poetry is a stronger, more potent version of everyday language. Poems make the reader re-experience something in a powerful way. —Michael Strelow is a published poet and Professor of English Literature at Willamette University.

TV Writer

Writing for television is very different from writing for print. For one thing you have to learn to write "for time"—your words have to fit the pictures in the story! I wrote for the evening news and I loved working on deadline. I also liked that every day was different. Nobody cares about yesterday's news—so you are always writing about something new.—Vicki Hambleton worked as a writer for both ABC News and NBC News for over ten years.

Editor

I enjoy editing because I love decision making. I like making the choices—you are confronted with an array of possible stories and an array of possible photographs, covers . . . . I love all the ingredients that go into making the magazine and putting all the pieces together. After making lots of decisions week after week as an editor, it's wonderful to take three or four weeks and dive deep into some other kind of subject and come out with a big story that may be on the cover of Time.—Claudia Wallis is an editor at Time for Kids and writer for Time magazine.

Journalist

I find it amazing that I actually get paid to talk with people I find so interesting, from Tony Hawk to J.K. Rowling. It's fun to share stories with young readers about the people they are most interested in. My job is filled and variety and fun.—Janis Campbell is a writer for "Yak's Corner," a syndicated newspaper feature for kids.

Playwright

When I am writing, even though I am alone in a room, my characters keep me company. This is one reason I like to write plays: I'm never lonely. I also love to spend time around other playwrights, as well as actors, directors, and designers. Playwriting suits me because it is the perfect combination of intense solitude (while I write the play) and concentrated periods of sociability (rehearsals and performances). I have stories to tell; I have worlds to invent; I have people to create. I can't think of anything else I'd rather do.—Bridget Carpenter is the author of many plays, including *Fall*, which won the Susan Smith Blackburn Prize in 2000.

Children's Book Writer

While I was a librarian I started thinking it would be neat to write a book. My friend Marcia and I started talking about books we liked and ones we didn't like and said "Oh, it would be easy to do that." So the next day, we sat down for twenty minutes during our lunch break—we would eat our lunches and write at the same time. About a year and a half later we had our first book published. I love writing for kids.—Debbie Dadey is the author of more than sixty books, including the *Adventures of the Bailey School Kids* series.

Freelance Writer

They say necessity is the mother of invention. That also applies to the birth of my freelance career. I was about to be a single mother and writing was all I knew how to do. But sending my babies off to daycare seemed like cutting off my right arm without anesthetic. So. . . I became a freelance writer. Luckily, a WORKING freelance writer. I started writing primarily (80%) for children's markets. Now it's about 50/50 children's/adult markets. I love my job because of the vast flexibility of subject matter. It's as if I'm always learning, always taking new steps forward, intellectually. The "Freelance University" offers one of the best and most diverse educations on the planet.—Kelly Milner Halls, freelance writer for *Highlights, Fox Kids,* and *Chicago Tribune KidNews*

Other Writing Careers

Here's a list of different careers that you might want to think about:

Novel writer

Sports writer

News writer for television or radio

Foreign correspondent

Freelance writer

Editor

Fashion reporter

Medical writer

Technical writer

Screenwriter

Playwright

Children's writer

Speechwriter

These are just some of the careers open to writers—there are many more. If you know a writer whom you admire, don't be afraid to get in touch with him or her. Ask them what they like about their job and how they got started. Many writers enjoy talking to aspiring authors and giving them encouragement. Partly that's because most writers really love what they do. There is nothing better than doing something that makes you feel happy and fulfilled (okay, and TALENTED)…and maybe someday even makes you rich and famous. Like anything else, a writing career takes work, but if you follow the examples in this book, you'll be well on your way to any writing career you choose!

For many careers you need years of training, but the great thing about being a writer is that you can do it at any age. You don't have to finish college or pass a bunch of tests before you can start. You can also change your form, style, and the market for your writing as often as you like. If you start out writing Sci-Fi/Fantasy, you are not stuck with it for life—there are plenty of other genres out there! And if you start out writing magazine articles, you can easily move on to writing novels, too. The more you live and have different experiences, the more you will have to write about!

YOUR LIFE AS WRITER

You're humming to yourself on the school bus, of all places, and your cheeks kind of hurt from all that smiling. You can't wait to get home and get this into your journal—and maybe try a new writing prompt, too. It was pretty amazing today when Mrs. Crabapple gave out copies of this month's Teen Ink in English and your short story was in it. There it was, your writing, and there was your name, in print. The whole class cheered. You know that not only do you wanna be a writer—you are a writer!

So, you wanna be a writer? Go for it!!! Look over this book and start anywhere you want—set up your writing space, get yourself a journal, try a new writing prompt, order a book, start a writing group, read a magazine with writing by young authors—these things that real writers do, and lots more, are right here for you. We said in the first chapter that if you like to write, you are one of the luckiest people in the world, and we meant it. It's something you can do right now, do for the rest of your life, love every minute of—and even get paid for! C' ya in print!

Kevin Shimkus, age 14

Kevin is a freshman in high school who recently won the honor of being published in *Celebration of Young Poets* by Creative Communications.

Do you have favorite styles of writing or subjects?
My poetry is strictly rhyming because this is the style of poetry I most enjoy reading myself. My favorite story that I've written is based on the children's crusades through France during the fifteenth century. The story is fictional, but in order to get the time and setting historically correct, I talked to a few of my school's history teachers. I call this style of writing "realistic fiction" and it's my favorite to write. Sometimes when I hear about a cool event that has happened in the past, I play off of that event to create my own stories with different names and adventures.

Do you have any special tools that aid you in your writing?
My best strategy for writing is not to write anything at all. I can never get the right words to come out when I am sitting over a piece of paper or hunched over a keyboard. I have lost great stories just because I could not type out my ideas fast enough or write everything I need to before it is forgotten. This had proved to be a huge problem for me until I found a great way to collect my ideas and bring them back—I bought a tape recorder. A very simple one, but whenever I was outside or in my room, an idea could emerge, and all I had to do was reach for my recorder and speak my mind.

It would help when I was in a place where pulling out a sheet of paper and a pen and sitting down was really illogical. I would title each idea to organize my thoughts and to give my mind an idea of what kind of sample was about to be played—a brief story plot, a great metaphor, a new color seen in the sunrise, or even an interesting word or saying on a billboard. I enjoy writing realistic fiction, and when I need to get an opinion, or I ask one question to a group of people and record their answers, or even have someone say a certain line to better the dialogue for my story, I can make use of my recorder. You can't carry your writer's desk everywhere with you, but you can carry a small, no-hassle black box that can become the library of your imagination.

CHAPTER 11

Resources for Writers

Maybe you know writers who can just sit down and write every day with no problems, but we don't! Most writers do lots of things to get their creative juices flowing, including taking writing courses, joining writing groups, reading books about writing, and using writing prompts for inspiration. Here are some of the wonderful books available that are particularly good for young writers. We have also given you some suggestions for different contests and magazine and book publishers that are interested in the writing of young adults. You'll find everything you need to know from contacts to websites to addresses!

GET MORE INFORMATION ON HOW TO BE A BETTER WRITER

Getting the Knack: 20 Poetry Writing Exercises. Stephen Dunning and William Stafford. Urbana, IL: National Council of Teachers of English, 1992.

These two authors are very respected contemporary poets and their book describes fun and interesting forms of poetry, like *pan-*

toums and *acrostics*, as well as wonderful techniques and prompts that can be used for other kinds of writing besides poetry.

Grammar Smart: A Guide to Perfect Usage (Princeton Review). Nell Goddin and Erik Palma, editors. New York: Villard Books, 1993.
All writers need and deserve a good grammar handbook.

The Teachers and Writers Handbook of Poetic Forms. Ron Padgett, editor. New York: Teachers & Writers, 2000.
Lists poetic forms alphabetically and includes a clear definition and description of each, plus poets who write in that form and sample poems.

Literary Cavalcade. Scholastic, 555 Broadway, New York, NY 10012-3999. www.scholastic.com
This monthly magazine is aimed at high school students who are serious about reading and writing. It publishes a variety of writing by new authors, famous authors, plus the winners of the annual Scholastic Art & Writing Awards. "The Journal Page" gives 3-4 great writing prompts in each issue.

Live Writing: Breathing Life into Your Words. Ralph Fletcher. New York: Avon Books, 1999.
Fletcher gives practical tips and suggestions that fit all kinds of writers, at all kinds of stages of their writing lives.

The Place My Words Are Looking For: What Poets Say About and Through Their Work. Paul Janeczko, Editor. New York: School Library and Binding, 1990.
Thirty-nine of our leading poets share their poetry as well as their thoughts, inspirations, anecdotes, and memories. The poems are

beautifully crafted, clear, and on a variety of subjects for all kinds of young adult readers. Each poet writes a few paragraphs about his or her writing, and about what life is like for a writer—a unique source of ideas about writing by real writers.

Scope. 555 Broadway, New York, NY 10012-3999. E-mail scopemag@scholastic.com, or website www.scholastic.com
 A monthly magazine for readers and writers in grades 6-9. The articles are on current events and movies, followed by interesting writing prompts.

Sleeping on the Wing: An Anthology of Modern Poetry With Essays on Reading and Writing. Kenneth Koch and Kate Farrell. New York: Vintage Books, 1982.
 An excellent collection of famous poets and their poems. You will learn how the poets got their ideas and about their techniques. Best of all, the book includes prompts for writing poems or stories based on some of the famous pieces.

Writers Inc: A Student's Handbook for Writing and Learning. Patrick Sebranek. Burlington, WI: Write Source Educational Publishing House, 1999.
 This easy to use and very comprehensive book has short, clear definitions and explanations for all areas of writing including grammar and usage, plus standard formats and content for different forms of writing. This is a book a writer can use in middle school, high school, college, and beyond.

A Writer's Notebook: Unlocking the Writer in You. Ralph Fletcher. New York: Avon Books, 1996.

This guide will show you exactly how to keep a writer's note-book, the most important tool a writer can have.

Writing! Weekly Reader Corporation, 900 Skokie Boulevard, Northbrook, IL 60062-4028. 1-847-205-3000 or 1-800-446-3355
This monthly magazine is for young writers in grades 7-12. It has articles about writers and writing, plus stories and poems. After each article, there is a "Write Now!" prompt based on the article. The magazine encourages readers to send in their writing for possible publication and sponsors annual writing contests.

Writing Smart: Your Guide to Great Writing (The Princeton Review). Marcia Lerner. New York: Villard Books, 1999.
This is a basic guide to writing that you can use as a reference for various forms and formats, as well as methods for citations, bibliography, etc.

Writing to Deadline: The Journalist at Work. Donald Murray. Portsmouth, NH: Heinemann, 2000.
If you are interested in nonfiction writing, this is the book for you. This books lets you into the real life of the journalist.

Writing Toward Home: Tales and Lessons to Find Your Way. Georgia Heard. Portsmouth, NH: Heinemann Boynton/Cook, 1995.
Over 55 different and fascinating writing prompts. By the time you finish reading just one of these prompts, you'll be itching to write.

Writing With Power: Techniques for Mastering the Writing Process. Peter Elbow. New York:Oxford University Press, 1981.
Elbow is a famous writing teacher who gives readers lists of great

writing topics and ideas for expanding your writing after you've gotten started.

Writing Your Own Plays: Creating, Adapting, Improvising. Carol Korty. New York: Players Press, 2000.

This book gives you practical tips and helpful examples to improve your play writing skills.

GET MORE INFORMATION ON HOW TO GET PUBLISHED

Go Public! Encouraging Student Writers to Publish. Susanne Rubenstein. Urbana, IL: National Council of Teachers of English, 1998.

Not just for teachers, this guide offers specific writing ideas and activities to help young writers develop the confidence and the ability to get their writing published. Contains an extensive list of commercial markets and writing contests open to young people.

Market Guide for Young Writers: Where and How to Sell What You Write. Kathy Henderson. Whitehall, VA: Betterway Publications, 1996.

Gives detailed information on studying markets, authors' tips for writing and submitting, detailed instructions on writing and preparing manuscripts, and contest resources for young writers.

To Be a Writer: A Guide for Young People Who Want to Write and Publish. Barbara Seuling. Breckenridge, CO: Twenty-First Century Books, 1997.

This book offers detailed how-to information on writing from start to finish, as well as lists of publishers (including e-zines) that accept the work of young writers. There is also information about contests, prizes, and writers' camps.

The Ultimate Guide to Student Contests, Grades 7-12. Scott Pendleton. New York: Walker & Co., 1997.

Describes over 400 national contest, programs, clubs, and more for young people. Includes essay-writing, filmmaking, and poetry contests, as well as academic contests for math, geography, art, and others. Check to make sure you get a recent edition— the contests change every year.

Writer's Market: Where and How to Sell What You Write
Poet's Market: Where and How to Publish Your Poetry Cincinnati, Ohio: Writer's Digest Books, 2000.

These directories are updated and issued in a new volume each year and are available at public libraries and book stores. Used by serious writers to locate all kinds of publishers and submission information, they contain thousands of listings of publishers, contests, and awards, as well as complete submission and contact information.

GET YOUR WRITING PUBLISHED

Magazines

The Apprentice Writer (grades 9-12). Short stories, personal experience essays, profiles, poems, and photo essays are all published in this annual. It is distributed to schools in the Middle Atlantic states. Contact: *The Apprentice Writer*, P.O. Box GG, Susquehanna University, Selinsgrove, PA 17870-1001. Web: www.susqu.edu

Cicada (ages 14-21). This magazine comes out six times a year and features fiction and book reviews for young adults. Stories from readers are welcome. Contact: Submissions Editor, *Cicada Magazine*, P.O. Box 300, Peru, IL 61354. www.cricketmag.com

The Claremont Review (ages 13-19). A literary journal targeted for young adult writers in North America. Fiction, poetry, and short plays are judged according to maturity of content and evidence of meticulous editing. Contact: The Claremont Review Publishers, 4980 Wesley Road, Victoria, BC, CANADA V8Y 1Y9. Web: www.claremont.sd63.bc.ca

Creative Kids (ages 8-14). An opportunity for children to share their creative and expressive work in a publication that is read by thousands of readers. Contact: Prufrock Press, P.O. Box 8813, Waco, TX 76714-8813.

Cricket (ages 6-16). A different contest is announced in each month's issue. Genres vary: poetry, short story, nonfiction, art. Contact: Submissions Editor, *Cricket Magazine*, P.O. Box 300, Peru, IL 61354. Web: www.cricketmag.com

Cyberteens (ages 19 and younger). Teen writers and artists are featured on this e-zine. Stories, articles, poems, reviews of software, books, and music, and opinion pieces are all found on the site. Contact: *Cyberteens*, 1041 Lake Street, San Francisco, CA 94118. Web: www.cyberteens.com

Girls' Life (girls ages 10-15). This bimonthly magazine is available in libraries and stores and accepts all kinds of articles written by girls. Contact: Freelance Writing, Attn: Kelly White, *Girls' Life* Magazine,

4517 Harford Rd., Baltimore, MD 21214. Web: www.girlslife.com

Guideposts for Teens (ages 12-18). Advice, humor, and true stories are all found in this Christian magazine, published six times a year. The editors are always looking for true stories about or written by teens that offer a Christian point of view. Contact: *Guideposts for Teens,* P.O. Box 638, Chesterton, IN 46304. Web: www.gp4teens.com

High School Writer (grades 7-9). This national newspaper features student writing, but only accepts material from students of teachers who subscribe to the newspaper. Contact: *High School Writer*, Write Publications, P.O. Box 718, Grand Rapids, MI 55744-0718.

Kid's World (ages 2-18). This magazine publishes stories, jokes, riddles and artwork by writers and artists under age 18 and is edited by high school students. Contact: *Kid's World*, 1300 Kicker Road, Tuscaloosa, AL 35404.

Latingirl (girls ages 12-19). This magazine is published six times a year and publishes articles on education and social issues for Hispanic teens. Contact: *Latingirl*, 70 Hudson Street, Ste. 5, Hoboken, NJ 07030-5618. Web: www.latingirlmag.com

Literary Cavalcade (grades 9-12). Features articles and stories about contemporary literature, as well as showcase student writing. Contact: Scholastic Inc., 555 Broadway, New York, NY 10012. Web: www.teacher.scholastic.com/products/langarts.htm

Merlyn's Pen (grades 6-12). This annual magazine publishes fiction, poetry, essays, and reviews written by kids. They also sponsor a short story contest. You must include a $1 submission fee or $5 for an editor's critique. Contact: *Merlyn's Pen*, P.O. Box 910, East Greenwich, RI 02818. E-mail: merlynspen@aol.com or Web: www.merlynspen.com

New Moon: The Magazine for Girls and Their Dreams (girls ages 8-14). This bimonthly magazine is edited by and for girls and accepts letters, poems, stories, drawings, and jokes written by girls. Contact: *New Moon* Magazine, P.O. Box 3620, Duluth, MN 55803-3620. 1-218-728-5507 or Web: www.newmoon.org

Scholastic Scope Magazine (ages 12-19). Each issue includes an essay written by a kid about "the book that had a big effect on you." It also has a regular "Yes/No" column debating both sides of controversial topics. Readers are encouraged to send in opinions for publication in later issues. Contact: *Scholastic Scope*, 555 Broadway, New York, NY 10012-3999. E-mail: scopemag@scholastic.com or Web: www.scholastic.com

Skipping Stones (ages 8-16). This magazine welcomes articles on different cultures as well as fiction written by young authors. Contact: Managing Editor, *Skipping Stones*, P.O. Box 3939, Eugene, OR 97403-0939.

Sports Illustrated for Kids (ages 8-14). This monthly magazine uses opinion pieces written by young authors. Contact: Letters, *Sports Illustrated for Kids*, 1271 Avenue of the Americas, New York, NY 10020-1393. E-mail: kidletters@sikids.com or Web: www.sikids.com

Stone Soup (ages 6-14). Poetry, book reviews, artwork, and stories from contributors under the age of 14 are found in each issue of this magazine. Contact: *Stone Soup*, P.O. Box 83, Santa Cruz, CA 95063. Web: www.stonesoup.com

TeenInk (21st Century) (grades 7-12). This monthly newsprint magazine and quarterly poetry magazine that features fiction, poetry, nonfiction, reviews, and interviews by young authors. The *Chicken Soup for the Soul* publishers recently published a book of best pieces from *Teen Ink*. Contact: *Teen Ink*, P.O. Box 30, Newton, MA 02461. E-mail: editor@teenink.com or Web: www.teenink.com

Teen Voices Magazine (girls ages 12-19). This magazine is published quarterly by a multicultural volunteer group of teens and young adult women, and contains writing by and for young women to "provide an intelligent alternative to glitzy, gossipy, fashion-oriented publications that too often exploit the insecurities of their young audiences." Female readers are encouraged to submit all forms of writing. Contact: *Teen Voices,* c/o Women Express, Inc. P.O. Box 120-027, Boston, MA 02112-0027. Phone: 1-888-882-TEEN or Web: www.teenvoices.com

Writes of Passage (ages 12-19). This literary e-zine that features the work of teen writers. Fiction, interviews, profiles, and poetry are all found on the site. Contact: *Writes of Passage*, Editorial Department, P.O. Box 1935, Livingston, NJ 07039. Web: www.writes.org

Writing! (ages 7-12). This magazine encourages readers to send in writing of all genres for potential publication. It also sponsors several writing contests each year. Contact: Weekly Reader Corporation, 900 Skokie Boulevard, Northbrook, IL 60062. 1-800-446-3355 or Web: www.weeklyreader.com

Young People's Press Online (ages 14-21). This group is responsible for a number of websites for teens. They don't publish any fiction writing, but they do accept articles from young writers on nonfiction topics like writing, health, community service, and equality. Contact: *Young People's Press Online*, CCSJ/YPP, 110 Eglington Ave. W., Suite 200, Toronto, Ontario P1B 3W7, CANADA. Web: writeus@ypp.net

Young Voices (all ages). Students of all ages are paid and published for their stories, poems, essays, and art. Contact: Young Voices, 504 Garrison St. NE, Olympia, WA 98507.

Writing Contests

Baker's Plays High School Playwriting Contest. This contest runs every year and is designed to showcase the work of high school playwrights. **Deadline January 30**. Send SASE for contest rules and entry form. Contact: High School Playwriting Contest, BAKER'S PLAYS, P.O. BOX 699222, Quincy, MA 02269-9222.

Kay Snow Writing Awards. This annual contest features an award for students 18 and younger. **Deadline May 15**. Send SASE for additional information and guidelines. Contact: Willamette Writers, 9045 SW Barbur Boulevard, Suite 5A, Portland, OR 97219

National Council of Teachers of English (NCTE) Promising Young Writers Program. Ask your teacher about being nominated to participate in this prestigious program for students in grades 8-11. Students must submit a sample of their writing plus write an essay on a topic selected by NCTE. **Deadline January**. Contact: NCTE Promising Young Writers Program, 1111 W. Kenyon Rd., Urbana, IL 61801-1096. Tel. 1-217-328-3870 or Web: www.ncte.org

Scholastic Writing Awards. This is the contest for young writers and artists! Students in grades 7-12 can enter short stories, essays, dramatic scripts, poetry, science fiction, fantasy, humor, or writing portfolios. **Deadline January.** Contact: Scholastic Art & Writing Awards, 555 Broadway, NY, NY 10012. Tel. 1-212-343-6493 or Web: www.scholastic.com

Seventeen Magazine Fiction Contest. This contest is for young writers ages 13-21. Entries must be stories that will appeal to teens, are no longer than 4,000 words, and have not been published before. **Deadline April 30**. Request contest guidelines for more information. Contact: *Seventeen* Fiction Contest, 850 Third Avenue, New York, NY 10022 Web: www.seventeen.com

Book Publishers

Beyond Words Publishing, Inc. The company that published this book has also published hundreds of kid authors. With "declared values" that include "creativity and aesthetics nourish the soul" and "living your passion is vital," this publisher truly believes in getting young writers into print. They publish only nonfiction by young writers. Contact: Beyond Words Publishing, 20827 NW Cornell Rd., Suite 500, Hillsboro, OR 97124-9808. Phone: 1-800-284-9673, Web: www.beyondword.com, E-mail: submissions@beyondword.com

Creative With Words Publications. This company publishes anthologies of fiction and nonfiction for readers of all ages. Each anthology is based on a theme and includes material from young writers. Contact: Creative With Words Publications, P.O. Box 223226, Carmel, CA 93922. Web: www.members.tripod.com

May Davenport, Publishers. This company publishes fiction for grades K-12. It is especially interested in material for young adult readers. Contact: May Davenport, Publishers, 26313 Purissima Road, Los Altos Hills, CA 94022.
Web: www.maydavenportpublishers.com

Girl Press. This publishing company specializes in nonfiction books for teenage readers. Its list includes novelty books, biographies, and how-to titles. They do not publish any fiction writing. Contact: Girl Press, PO Box 480389, Los Angeles, CA 90048.
Web: www.girlpress.com

Tricycle Press. This company is dedicated to creating books that help kids understand themselves and the world around them. They accept both fiction and nonfiction by young writers. Contact: Tricycle Press, P.O. Box 7123, Berkeley, CA 94707.
Web: www.tenspeed.com

Charlie Feid, age 12

Charlie enjoys writing fiction stories taken from real life and from his dreams.
He advises using your favorite author as a model for your own writing. He has
entered writing contests from *Teen Ink* and *Voices from the Middle*.

Why do you enjoy writing?
I am in control of my own world, and by reading what I wrote I can create my
own world for myself and any others who want to join me.

What are your favorite books?
I have a few favorite books. One of them is *The Phantom Tollbooth*. I thought
it was a very creative and funny story, and I think the author, Norton Juster,
had a lot of fun writing it. It is a book about a kid who gets transported into
another world. Everything is strange and the book is about him exploring it. I
used this book as an idea starter for a story I wrote about a kid who finds a
chest in his grandpa's attic. When he opens the chest, there's a clear mirror and
he walks through it into another world.

How do you come up with your ideas?
I come up with my ideas by reading books and changing them. I also come up
with ideas by writing down my dreams. That is why I have so many stories that
I can always write about. Dream stories are a lot like the fantasy stories that I
like to read. I write down my dreams most mornings if I can remember them.
This method works well if you take the time to write it down.

This is an excerpt from Charlie's novel, *John Marson*:

As quick as it could possibly come, four years had passed. Everything was supposedly ready. I was doing a checklist to make sure.

"Astro-Fibolic space helmets" I said.

"Check," said one of the workmen.

"Fiberoptibonic space capsule"

"Check"

"Tubyolic round ended rockets"

"Check"

"Dummies"

"Check"

"All right people. We're ready for a test run. Bring in the heavy technology."

Five workmen jumped out and wheeled the machine in. It was a beautiful sight. It looked like snow on Christmas morning, or the outcome of something you had been saving up to buy. It was too beautiful for words. It said the word "Firebolt" on the side. I pressed the startup button on the control panel in the control room outside the capsule. "Brrrrrrrr" it sounded as it started up.

Just then the red phone rang. The red phone was the phone that our spy in Russia used. I picked it up.

"John" the secret agent said "it's Special Agent #2. Russia is launching their spacecraft in only four hours! That's all I can tell you, someone may be tapping the phone. Bye."

"Cancel the test run!" I commanded. "Load the supplies!"

In three hours it was ready to go. I put my space suit on and got in with George.

"This is our day, George. This is the day we have been waiting for since we were kids," I said.

We closed the door on the capsule.

"Firebolt, do you read?"

"We read you Starcommand," we both said at the same time.

"Liftoff in 10, 9, 8, 7, 6, 5, 4, 3, 2, 1, LIFTOFFFFFFFF!"

The engines roared as they spit fire out of them like they were gulping down Tabasco sauce. Higher and higher and higher we went until we were finally in orbit.

"Bedford, we are in orbit. I repeat, we are in orbit."

"We read you Firebolt."

CHAPTER 12

Glossary:
Words that Writers, Publishers, and Teachers Use A Lot...and What They Mean!

abstract: cannot be touched, tasted, smelled, heard, or seen (as opposed to something concrete, which *can* be perceived by one of the five senses). Emotions or ideas are abstract: love, hate, envy, greed, happiness, depression, anger, revenge, confidence, evil, kindness. (ch. 5)

acrostic: a poem that spells a word or phrase vertically, based on the first letter of each line. (ch. 5)

advance: a payment from a publisher when a writer signs a contract for a book. The advance is part of a writer's royalty payment, paid up front and deducted from later royalty payments. (ch. 9)

archetype: a model that is used over and over in literature. One example of an archetype is the classic hero (or heroine): an unlikely hero, called upon to go on a journey, encounters dangers, gathers friends, is helped by someone older and wiser, is successful because of cleverness and goodness rather than brute strength, returns home with a new understanding that is not always appreciated.(ch. 3)

autobiography: the story of a real person's life, written by the person herself. (ch. 3)

biography: the story of a real person's life, written by another person. (ch. 3)

bibliography: a list of the sources that an author used to write a book or research paper.

Call for Manuscripts: an advertisement that invites writers to submit writing by a certain date, usually on a specific topic or in a specific genre. Magazines often have their "Call for Manuscripts" in the front or back pages. Publishers and magazines insert their "Calls" in writing magazines, *Writer's Market* books, and on their websites.

character: a person (not necessarily human) who takes part in the action of a literary work. (ch. 6)

characterization: the act of creating and developing a character by:
1. direct description
2. dialogue—what the character says or what other characters say about him
3. actions—what the character does or what others do around the character

cite or **citation**: *to cite* is to include a very short note, or *citation* that gives the name of an author and title of the work from which you are using words or ideas. Citation is included in the text of a writing piece and in a bibliography. (ch. 6)

climax: the high point of interest or suspense in a story; the point at which the conflict is revealed. Some call the climax the *turning point* in a piece of writing. (ch. 6)

conflict: a struggle between opposing forces. *Internal conflict* occurs within the character's heart or mind. *External conflict* occurs between a character and an outside force: another character, or a force of nature (animal, weather, flood, disease, etc.). (ch. 6)

contract: a contract is a legal agreement between a publisher and an author. (ch. 9)

cover letter: a letter that you send with your manuscript, introducing yourself and your writing. (ch. 8)

dialogue: words said out loud in a conversation. When you write dialogue, use a book by a good author as a model for how to punctuate. (ch. 3, 5)

diary: a book in which you write about the events and ideas that occur in your life. Also called a journal. (ch. 2)

draft: any piece of writing that is not ready to send to a publisher or contest. A *rough draft* is writing in its earliest stages that you still plan to revise. A *final draft* has gone through revisions and editing so that it is finally ready to send out. Most writers number and date each draft. If you write directly on the computer, just put the date as part of the file name each time you save changes. Save hard copies of all drafts—you might use stuff you cut out in something else later on. (ch. 4)

editor: an editor makes suggestions to the author for additions, deletions, and reorganization in his or her writing so that it flows more logically and effectively for the reader. (ch. 6, 9)

epilogue: a concluding section that comes after the end of a work. An epilogue often summarizes the final results in the future for most or all characters. (ch. 5)

exposition: comes at the beginning of a piece of writing; the exposition introduces the reader to characters, setting, and conflict. An exposition is also a form of writing (expository writing) that is written to inform, compare, contrast, analyze, give cause and effect, or give how-to instructions. (ch. 6)

fable: a piece of fiction that teaches a lesson or a moral. Animal fables give animals human characteristics: the animals speak and act like human beings, and often show human emotions, virtues, and vices. (ch. 5) See *personification*.

found poem: a poem fashioned from someone else's writing (with the source cited). Usually, the original writing was NOT meant to be poetic, but the poet's artful choices, deletions, and re-arrangement make a new kind of meaning and sense. (ch. 5)

free writing: writing that is meant to get ideas and thoughts on paper with no concern for spelling, punctuation, grammar, sentence structure, paragraphs, or even staying on topic. (ch. 4)

genre: kind of writing. (ch. 2, 3)

guidelines: Guidelines tell you about a publisher's editorial needs and desires and can include genre, subject matter, word length, and reading level. (ch. 8)

inciting incident: an event in the beginning of a story, play, or narrative that introduces the conflict. (ch. 6)

journal: a book in which you write thoughts, observations, ideas, or anything that strikes you. Also called a diary. (ch. 2)

manuscript: a complete piece of original writing. Publishers and contests have guidelines for manuscripts that they publish. (ch. 8)

market: the intended audience of a piece of writing. (ch. 8)

memoir: autobiographical writing based on the writer's memories, usually written in the first person ("I"). (ch. 3)

metaphor: a figure of speech in which one thing is spoken of as if it were something else. Example: *Happiness is a warm puppy*. (ch. 5, 6)

models: Writers use books, stories, plays, and authors as models for their ideas and styles. Models can also be used to answer questions about punctuating dialogue or writing a bibliography. (ch. 3, 5)

monologue: a long speech spoken by one person. (ch. 3, 5) *plagiarism*: using someone else's words or ideas in your writing, without giving credit to the real author. Plagiarism is a serious offense—students who plagiarize can get expelled from school, adults who plagiarize can get fired from their jobs, and authors who plagiarize can get sued. It comes from the Latin word meaning to kidnap or abduct for ransom—plagiarists kidnap the words of others for their own benefit. (ch. 6)

plot: a sequence of events—beginning, middle, and end—in a piece of writing. (ch. 6)

point of view: the perspective or vantage point from which a story is told. There is the first person point of view ("I"); the second person point of view ("you"—usually only found in how-to writing), and the third person point of view ("they/he/she/it"). (ch. 6, 7)

prologue: a description of characters or events that have happened before the first chapter of a story. (ch. 5)

prompt: a short lesson or a few paragraphs that are meant to stimulate you as a writer and help you get started writing something. (ch. 4, 5)

query: a query is a letter sent to a publisher that describes the proposal and outlines an author's qualifications to write the article or book. (ch. 8)

rights: when a publisher buys a manuscript, they are buying the right to publish that manuscript. (ch. 9)

reader: someone who reads a piece of writing and responds to it so that the writer can find out what his or her potential audience might get from a particular piece. (ch. 7)

revise: to change an earlier draft in some way that affects the content: adding or inserting, deleting, combining sentences, moving around paragraphs, and rewriting parts in new ways to decide which way the writer likes best. With each revision, the writing should get better, more organized, and more interesting. (ch. 4, 6)

royalty: a publisher pays a writer a percentage of the cover price for each copy of the author's book that is sold. (ch. 9)

SASE: **S**elf **A**ddressed **S**tamped **E**nvelope. An envelope that has your name, address, and enough postage on it for the publisher to return your manuscript (if you want it back), or for the publisher to send back a note saying your submission was received—or accepted! (ch. 8)

theme: the central message an author wants to convey in his/her writing. In most literature, the theme is not directly stated, but can be implied by the reader. Theme is different from *moral*, which is a lesson that is usually stated directly at the end of the story. (ch. 5)

writer's guidelines: see guidelines.

writing group: a group of writers who meet regularly to learn about writing, and share, respond to, and critique each other's writing. (ch. 7)

About the Authors

Vicki Hambleton works full-time as a freelance writer and editor. She has worked on the staff of many magazines, including *Mademoiselle, US Weekly,* and *Good Housekeeping,* and written for many more. She also spent more than ten years working as a writer and a producer for both ABC News and CBS News. During her time in television network news she covered such stories as the wedding of Charles and Diana, the early space shuttle missions, the political primaries for the 1980 and 1984 elections, and several presidential inaugurations. Her work can be seen regularly in the magazines of Cobblestone Publishing: *Cobblestone, Calliope, Faces,* and *Footsteps.* She started a regional magazine on equestrian sports and she has also just launched a national newsletter for parents entitled *Parenting TEENS.* She lives in New York with her 15-year-old daughter who is also a published writer.

Cathleen Greenwood is a published writer, teacher, and speaker at professional conferences in teaching and writing. Her students have won awards, recognition, and/or published writing in The Scholastic Art & Writing Awards, *Teen Ink/21st Century, High School Writer, Scope, Cricket, Voices from the Middle,* NCTE Promising Young Writers Awards Program, *Merlyn's Pen, Teen Voices,* and Westchester Council of English Educators Young Writers' Contest. Cathy has published poems, short stories, and essays in *The Vineyard Gazette, English Journal* (NCTE), *English Record* (NYSEC) and *AIM* magazine, and is finishing a Masters in the Art of Writing from Northeastern University's Martha Vineyard Summer Workshops. She has received the Channel Thirteen "Telly" Award, the New York State English Council's Educator of Excellence Award, and Honorable Mention in Poetry from *English Journal.* Cathy teaches at the Rippowam Cisqua School in New York, is an executive board member of the New York State English Council, and loves to see young writers in print.

Notes

Notes

Notes

Notes

148

Notes

Other Books by Beyond Words Publishing

EVER IMAGINE CREATING YOUR OWN COMIC BOOKS?
Why just imagine? Make it happen!
Get great tips on:
- Starting a studio and choosing the right tools
- Creating your own characters and stories
- Developing your drawing techniques
- Submitting and selling your comics

Written by the editor of Dark Horse Comics, Phil Amara, with advice from other comic book professionals and kids who are currently getting their work noticed, *So, You Wanna Be a Comic Book Artist?* will tell you how to turn your love of comic books into a career. It doesn't matter if you're just beginning or have been drawing your own comics for years. ANYONE can create their own comic books—let your imagination soar!

144 pages, black and white art, $9.95 softcover

IS THERE A ROCK STAR IN THE HOUSE?
It could be you! All you budding musicologists, get the scoop on:
- Choosing the perfect name for your band
- Finding song ideas
- Creating a demo tape

✳ Scholastic & Book of the Month Club Selection ✳

How did Britney Spears get her start? This book won't tell you that, but it will inspire you to live your rock and roll dream: from how to start a band, to how to get discovered, and everything in between (like finding the perfect look and attitude to express your musical soul, and, of course, getting your parents on board to the whole idea of you as a rock star). Written by a former teenage rocker, with advice from twenty real kid bands. Rock on!

152 pages, black and white art, $8.95 softcover

HEY BOYS! WHY WAIT FOR SUCCESS?

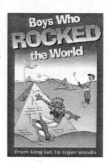

Did you know:

- Galileo invented the first accurate mechanical clock at the age eighteen?

- Louis Braille created an alphabet system for the blind when he was only fifteen?

- Bill Gates founded his first computer company and invented a machine to solve traffic problems at sixteen?

Boys Who Rocked the World shares the stories of boys who have made a difference in the world before the age of twenty and also profiles boys currently preparing to take the world by storm. Now it's your turn! The world is waiting to be rocked!

160 pages, black and white art, $8.95 softcover

GREAT STORIES OF REAL GIRLS WHO MADE HISTORY!

Did you know that:

- Joan of Arc was only 17 when she led the French troops to victory?

- Cristen Powell started drag racing at 16 and is now one of the top drag racers in America?

- Wang Yani began painting at the age of three? She was the youngest artist ever to have her own exhibit at the Smithsonian museum!

✳ Scholastic & Book of the Month Club Selection ✳

Girls Who Rocked the World lets you get to know these incredible teen-age girls and many more. This is the first book ever to set girls' history straight by telling the stories of inspiring young heroines.

Impress your girlfriends with even more great stories of women heroines with *Girls Who Rocked the World 2.*

✳ A Troll Book Club Selection ✳

So . . . how are you going to rock the world?

160 pages, black and white illustrations, $8.95 softcover

Everywhere you turn, teen magazines are telling you how to look and who you're supposed to be. Shouldn't YOU be the authority on yourself? Sixteen-year-old Sarah Stillman offers an escape from superficiality in her book *Soul Searching: A Girl's Guide to Finding Herself.*

Learn how to:
- Create a calming atmosphere for yourself through Feng Shui and Aromatherapy
- Relax with yoga and meditation
- Keep a journal and analyze your dreams
- Find your passions and accomplish your goals

It's time to start discovering yourself—you never know what you might find!

140 pages, black and white art, $10.95 softcover

DOES YOUR MEOWER HAVE PSYCHIC POWER? DOES FIDO KNOW THINGS YOU DON'T KNOW?

Do you dare to explore the uncharted world of your pet's brain? Read about:

- Spooky stories of pets with psychic powers
- Tests to find out if your pet is psychic
- Ways to increase your pet's psychic abilities
- Astrology charts for your pet

✳ Scholastic & Book of the Month Club Selection ✳

Can your cat get out of the house even when all the doors are closed? Has your dog ever seen a ghost? Does your horse seem to read your mind? If you can answer yes to any of these questions, you might have (are you sitting down?) a psychic pet! Better keep that food dish filled from now on!

124 pages, black and white art, $7.95 softcover

KIDSMAKINGMONEY.COM

Okay, *Better Than a Lemonade Stand,* by fifteen-year-old author Daryl Bernstein, is not a guide to high tech riches. But computers aren't the only way to get rich quick. Daryl started his first business when he was only eight! Since then, he has tried all fifty-one of the kid

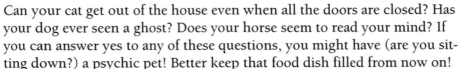

businesses in this book, all of which are easy to start up. Today, Daryl runs his own multimillion-dollar business and is happy to share with you the secrets of his success. Learn how you can earn bucks by being a:

- baby-sitting broker

- dog walker

- mural painter and many, many more fun money making jobs!!!

✳ A Doubleday Book Club Selection ✳

150 pages, black and white cartoon illustrations, $9.95 softcover

EXCUSES! EXCUSES!

Authors Mike and Zach are excuse experts. These nine- and ten-year-old best friends have created *100 Excuses for Kids*, a hysterical book which will give you great excuses for getting out of anything vegetables, homework, chores whatever! Get the latest and newest excuses for:

- Going to bed late

- Not eating your vegetables

- Not cleaning your room and many (97 to be exact), many more!

✳ Scholastic Book Club Selection ✳

96 pages, black and white cartoon art, $5.95 softcover

HEY, GUYS!
EVERYTHING YOU NEED TO KNOW, ACCORDING TO THE "EXPERTS"—GUYS JUST LIKE YOU!

Read about:

- tips on catching frogs, bugs, and other creatures

- wise-cracks to make your buddies laugh

- being the best big brother

- the scoop on girls

From making comic strips to dealing with girls, *Boys Know It All* is packed with great ideas from thirty-two cool guys —just like you!

160 pages, black and white collage art, $8.95 softcover

HEY, GIRLS!
SPEAK OUT • BE HEARD • BE CREATIVE •
GO FOR YOUR DREAMS!

Discover how you can:

- handle grouchy, just plain ornery adults

- pass notes in class without getting caught

- avoid life's most embarrassing moments

＊ Scholastic & Book of the Month Club Selection ＊

Girls Know Best celebrates girls' unique voices and wisdom. 38 girls, ages 7-15, share their advice and activities. Everything you need to know... from the people who've been there: girls just like you!

160 pages, black and white collage art, $8.95 softcover

LISTEN UP!
GIRLS HAVE MORE TO SAY!

More girl wisdom on:

- how to have the best slumber party ever

- discovering the meanings of your dreams

- overcoming any obstacle, whenever, wherever

160 pages, black and white collage art, $8.95 softcover

GIRLS CANNOT BE SILENCED!
EVEN MORE GIRL TALK!

Answers all your questions about:

- different religions

- starting your own rock band

- whether alternative schooling is for you and, of course, much, much more!

132 pages, black and white collage art, $8.95 softcover

YOU GO GIRL!

Learn how to master your:

- Body: feeding and training your incredible machine

- Mind: talking yourself into sports success

- Spirit: dealing with others' negativity

Throw Like a Girl gives you information and inspiration to get involved in sports: for fun, for fitness, and even for a career. Hear from the experts, the stars, and from girls like you. Learn about sports nutrition and exercises while you're picking up tips for dealing with pushy coaches, teammates, and, oh yes, even parents.

160 pages, black and white collage art, $10.95 softcover

GROWING UP JUST GOT A LITTLE EASIER

Life can be tough, especially when you're in between everything. *The Girls Life Guide to Growing Up* helps relieve the stress of "tweendom" and "teendom" and shows you how to deal with:

- She's All That—Or is She? The myths of hangin' with the "in" crowd are busted by girls who have been there.

- What Kind of Smart Are You? Intelligence is more than a grade on a math test. This quiz reveals your true talents.

- Whose Body Is This, Anyway? Yeah, you're going through some crazy changes. Know what to expect and how to cope.

✳ Scholastic Book Club Selection ✳

It's as cool an advice book as you'll ever want, written by the staff of your favorite magazine, Girls Life. Take the quizzes, read the chapters and become self aware! See what guys really think about all this girl stuff, and laugh out loud as you read about everything girl, from friends, family, crushes, school, your body, and most of all, you!

272 pages, black and white illustrations, $11.95 softcover

TO ORDER ANY OF THE BOOKS LISTED HERE OR TO REQUEST A CATALOG, PLEASE CONTACT US OR MAIL US THIS ORDER FORM.

Name _____

Address _____

City _____ State/Province _____ Zip/Postal Code _____

Country _____

Phone Number _____

Title	Quantity	Price	Line Total
_____			
_____			
_____			
_____			
_____			
_____			

Subtotal _____

Shipping (see below) _____

Total _____

We accept Visa, MasterCard, and American Express, or send a check or money order payable to Beyond Words Publishing.

Credit Card Number _____ Exp. Date _____

Shipping Rates (within the United States only)
First book: $3.00   Each additional book: $1.00
Please call for special shipping services (overnight or international).

Beyond Words Publishing, Inc.
20827 NW Cornell Road, Suite 500
Hillsboro, OR 97124-9808

or contact us by phone:
(503) 531-8700
fax: (503) 531-8773
email: sales@beyondword.com